Phonics for Teachers

Phonics for Teachers

Self-Instruction, Methods, and Activities

J. Lloyd Eldredge

Brigham Young University

MERRILL
an imprint of Prentice Hall
Upper Saddle River, New Jersey   Columbus, Ohio

Library of Congress Cataloging-in-Publication Data

Eldredge, J. Lloyd (Joseph Lloyd)
　Phonics for teachers : self-instruction, methods, and activities /
by J. Lloyd Eldredge.
　　p.　　cm.
　Includes index.
　ISBN 0-13-259425-0
　1. Reading—Phonetic method. 2. Reading—Phonetic method-
-Problems, exercises, etc.　3. Education, Elementary—Activity
programs. I. Title.
LB1573.3.E427　1999
372.46'5—dc21　　　　　　　　　　　　　98-17012
　　　　　　　　　　　　　　　　　　　　　　CIP

Cover art: © Stephen R. Schildbach
Editor: Bradley J. Potthoff
Production Editor: Mary M. Irvin
Production Coordination: Linda Zuk, WordCrafters Editorial Services, Inc.
Text Designer: Linda Zuk
Cover Designer: Dan Eckel
Design Coordinator: Diane C. Lorenzo
Production Manager: Pamela D. Bennett
Director of Marketing: Kevin Flanagan
Marketing Manager: Suzanne Stanton
Advertising/Marketing Coordinator: Krista Groshong

This book was set in Bookman by Carlisle Communications Ltd. and was printed and bound by R.R. Donnelley & Sons Company. The cover was printed by Phoenix Color Corp.

 © 1999 by Prentice-Hall, Inc.
Simon & Schuster/A Viacom Company
Upper Saddle River, New Jersey 07458

Printed in the United States of America

10　9　8　7　6　5　4

ISBN: 0-13-259425-0

Prentice-Hall International (UK) Limited, *London*
Prentice-Hall of Australia Pty. Limited, *Sydney*
Prentice-Hall of Canada, Inc., *Toronto*
Prenticc-Hall Hispanoamcricana, S. A., *Mexico*
Prentice-Hall of India Private Limited, *New Delhi*
Prentice-Hall of Japan, Inc., *Tokyo*
Simon & Schuster Asia Pte. Ltd., *Singapore*
Editora Prentice-Hall do Brasil, Ltda., *Rio de Janeiro*

Preface

Reading and writing are processes that require certain knowledge and thinking abilities. For effective reading and writing, we need a working knowledge of encoding/decoding, vocabulary, syntax, and discourse. Writing requires an ability to represent (encode) spoken language by using the symbols designated for this purpose, and reading requires an ability to translate written language into spoken language (decode). Writers need to be able to select appropriate words (vocabulary/schemata) and sentence patterns (syntax) to communicate their ideas to readers, and readers must possess the necessary schemata, vocabulary, and syntax knowledge to understand what writers are trying to communicate. Writers need to be able to connect important ideas between sentences *and* larger units of text (discourse knowledge), and readers must be able to perceive these idea relationships.

Both readers and writers must be able to think. Effective writers use their encoding, schemata, vocabulary, syntax, and discourse knowledge to entertain, teach, and create visual images from written words. Effective readers do more than merely read the lines of text. They read between the lines to perceive relationships among ideas, to create their own visual images as they read; and they read beyond the lines of text so they can critically evaluate the messages writers create.

Reading is a process involving much more than decoding. However, without the ability to translate the written language into spoken language, readers could not "read." Without the ability to decode, individuals could not access their vocabulary, syntax, schemata, or discourse knowledge to construct meaning from written text. In short, vocabulary, syntax, schemata, and discourse knowledge are used by readers when they engage in the higher-order thinking processes associated with effective reading comprehension. However, these sources of knowledge cannot be accessed without automatic, fluent decoding. Decoding knowledge, therefore, is an essential first step in the reading process.

The focus of this text is decoding. The major portion of this book is organized as a self-instruction text to help you understand phonics and its role in the enhancement of decoding processes and overall reading growth. Phonics knowledge is needed for the identification of words by analogy and by context. It is necessary for "sounding out" both single and multisyllabic words. It is also needed for identifying words by morphemic analysis. Furthermore, existing research reveals that phonics knowledge is needed for extensive word recognition. Since word recognition is necessary for reading fluency, and reading fluency is essential for reading comprehension, phonics knowledge is extremely important.

The latter portion of this book is devoted to phonics teaching. In this portion of the book, you will be introduced to teaching activities that direct children's attention toward written words so they can discover how speech sounds are mapped onto print. These activities are designed to help children learn strategies for identifying written words they don't recognize and, in the process, enhance their word recognition abilities.

This text can be used in college courses, in-service workshops, and independently by individuals who wish to improve their understanding and use of phonics.

Acknowledgments

We would like to thank the reviewers of the manuscript for their insightful comments: Patricia P. Fritchie, Troy State University–Dothan; Edward W. Holmes, Towson State University; Nancy B. Keller, State University of New York–Oneonta; William S. O'Bruba, Bloomsburg University; and Nancy H. Phillips, Lynchburg College.

About the Author

J. Lloyd Eldredge is a professor in the College of Education at the Brigham Young University, where he teaches both graduate and undergraduate literacy courses.

Dr. Eldredge is a former elementary school teacher, school principal, and school superintendent. He has also served as the Utah Director of Chapter I, the Utah Director of Early Childhood Education, and the Utah Director of Elementary Education.

During the past 14 years his research has been focused on phonemic awareness, phonics, a reconceptualization of decoding instruction in the early years of schooling, whole language, oral reading, and the effects of various forms of "assisted reading" strategies (dyad reading, group assisted reading, and taped assisted reading) on young and "at risk" readers. His work is published in such journals as *Journal of Educational Research, Reading Research and Instruction, Journal of Reading, The Reading Teacher, Journal of Literacy Research,* and *Reading Research Quarterly.* He is the author of two books on phonics and decoding: *Decoding Strategies* and *Teaching Decoding in Holistic Classrooms.*

Contents

Self-Evaluation: A Pretest ———

This is a test to give you an indication of your present knowledge of phonics and issues related to it. Read each item carefully, including all of the choices. Circle the letter (a, b, c, d, or e) to indicate your best answer. Be sure to respond to all test items.

I. Multiple Choice. Select the best answer.

1. How many phonemes are in the word *stretch?*

   a. one   **b.** two   **c.** five   **d.** six   **e.** seven

2. How many graphemes are in the word *stretch?*

   a. one   **b.** two   **c.** five   **d.** six   **e.** seven

3. Which of the following most adequately completes the sentence? The meanings young readers acquire from reading are largely based on

   a. written context.
   b. prosody.
   c. decoding.
   d. their knowledge of spoken words.
   e. phonics.

4. Which of the following most adequately completes the sentence? The written language is

   a. difficult to understand.
   b. as easy to acquire as the oral language.
   c. used more often in schools than the oral language.
   d. a representation of the oral language.
   e. a primary language form.

5. Which of the following most adequately completes the sentence? Language can be

   a. either associative or communicative.
   b. either expressive or receptive.
   c. either oral or written.
   d. All of the above.
   e. Both b and c.

6. Which of the following most adequately completes the sentence? The major reason we study phonics is to

   a. learn about consonant and vowel sounds.
   b. learn how to "sound out" words.
   c. learn how the spoken language relates to the written language.
   d. become phonemically aware.
   e. Both b and c.

7. Which of the following most adequately completes the sentence? The differences in the meanings that we associate with spoken words are affected mostly by

 a. graphemes.
 b. phonemes.
 c. syllables.
 d. phonological awareness.
 e. syntax.

8. Which of the following most adequately completes the sentence? If we didn't have a written language, there would be little reason to

 a. learn about syntax.
 b. study phonics.
 c. develop phonemic awareness.
 d. learn about text structure.
 e. Both b and c.

9. Which of the following statement/s are correct?

 a. A phoneme is the written representation of a grapheme.
 b. A grapheme is the written representation of a phoneme.
 c. A phoneme is the smallest unit of sound in a word.
 d. *Grapheme* and *letter* are synonymous terms.
 e. Statements b and c are correct.

10. Which of the following statement/s are correct?

 a. The letter *x* has no sound of its own.
 b. The letter *c* has no sound of its own.
 c. The letters *y* and *w* are used to represent both consonant and vowel phonemes.
 d. The letter *q* has no sound of its own.
 e. All of the statements above are correct.

11. The letter *y* is most likely to be a consonant when

 a. it is the first letter in a word or syllable.
 b. it is the final letter in a word or syllable.
 c. it occurs in the middle of a syllable.
 d. it follows the letter *a* in a word or syllable.
 e. None of the above.

12. Which of the following most adequately completes the sentence? Most of the consonant speech sounds are predictably represented by

 a. 18 consonant letters and 5 consonant digraphs.
 b. 21 consonant letters.
 c. single-letter consonants and consonant blends.
 d. 21 consonant phonemes.
 e. The written form of the American English language is too irregular for any safe predictions.

13. The consonant digraph is illustrated by

    a. the *ai* in *rain.*
    b. the *sh* in *wish.*
    c. the *str* in *strap.*
    d. the *nd* in *bend.*
    e. the *gh* in *brought.*

14. The voiced equivalent of the consonant sound represented by the *p* in *pie* is

    a. the consonant sound represented by the *d* in *dog.*
    b. the consonant sound represented by the *b* in *bug.*
    c. the consonant sound represented by the *g* in *go.*
    d. the consonant sound represented by the *v* in *van.*
    e. the consonant sound represented by the *z* in *zoo.*

15. The voiceless equivalent of the consonant sound represented by the *j* in *job* is

    a. the consonant sound represented by the *f* in *fun.*
    b. the consonant sound represented by the *s* in *sit.*
    c. the consonant sound represented by the *ch* in *chin.*
    d. the consonant sound represented by the *t* in *top.*
    e. the consonant sound represented by the *c* in *can.*

16. Which of the following most adequately completes the sentence? Consonant phonemes and graphemes are

    a. used in the middle of syllables.
    b. used at the beginning and ending of syllables.
    c. more important than vowel phonemes and graphemes.
    d. Both a and b.
    e. None of the above.

17. Which of the following most adequately completes the sentence? The consonant letter *q* is not really needed to represent consonant phonemes because

    a. it never occurs in words without the letter *u* after it.
    b. other letters represent the sound/s it represents.
    c. it looks too much like the letter *g.*
    d. Both a and b.
    e. All of the above.

18. The consonant letter *s* most frequently represents the sound/s heard in

    a. *shall.*   **b.** *zipper.*   **c.** *sure.*   **d.** *sun.*   **e.** Both b and d

19. The word *stuff* ends with the same sound as the sound represented by

    a. the *f* in *of.*
    b. the *ph* in *graph.*
    c. the *gh* in *caught.*
    d. the *gh* in *ghost.*
    e. Both a and b.

20. The consonant letter *c* followed by an *e* is most likely to represent the same sound represented by

    a. the letter *c* in *cello*.
    b. the letter *s* in *sit*.
    c. the letter *c* when followed by *o*.
    d. the letter *c* when followed by *i*.
    e. Both b and d.

21. The consonant letter *g* followed by a *u* is most likely to represent the same sound represented by

    a. the *j* in *just*.
    b. the *gh* in *ghetto*.
    c. the *g* in *sing*.
    d. the letter *g* followed by *i*.
    e. Both a and d.

22. The open syllable in the nonsense word *pabel* would most likely rhyme with

    a. *crab*.
    b. *stay*.
    c. *fell*.
    d. *babe*.
    e. *rub*.

23. A vowel diphthong is best illustrated by the vowels representing the sound of

    a. *oo* as in *book*.
    b. *ou* as in *out*.
    c. *ai* as in *plaid*.
    d. *oy* as in *boy*.
    e. Both b and d.

24. The schwa sound is represented by

    a. the *o* in *lemon*.
    b. the *ay* in *day*.
    c. the *e* in *the*.
    d. the *e* in *wished*.
    e. Both a and c.

25. An example of a closed syllable is found in which of the following words?

    a. *bone*
    b. *go*
    c. *stand*
    d. *high*
    e. *see*

26. Which of the following has an incorrect diacritical mark?

    a. *wãll*   **b.** *sŏft*   **c.** *ūs*   **d.** *bĕd*   **e.** *bĭg*

27. Which of the following has an incorrect diacritical mark?

    a. *ūse*   **b.** *ēve*   **c.** *dīme*   **d.** *glōve*   **e.** *pāge.*

28. When the single vowel *u* is followed by a single consonant and a final *e*, the *u* would most likely have the sound of

    a. the *u* in *rude.*
    b. the *ew* in *few.*
    c. the *u* in *guest.*
    d. the *oo* in *moon.*
    e. Both a and d.

29. If the vowel *o* was the only and final vowel in a syllable, the *o* would most likely represent the same sound as

    a. the *o* in *other.*
    b. the *a* in *water.*
    c. the *o* in *to.*
    d. the *ough* in *dough.*
    e. None of the above.

30. If the single vowel *a* was in a syllable ending with one or more consonants, the *a* would most likely represent the same sound as

    a. the *ea* in *steak.*
    b. the *ai* in *said.*
    c. the *a* in *fall.*
    d. the *au* in *laugh.*
    e. None of the above.

31. The word containing a murmur diphthong is

    a. *trout.*
    b. *boy.*
    c. *first.*
    d. *cow.*
    e. *coin.*

32. When the letters *ai* appear together in a syllable, they usually represent the same sound as

    a. the *a* in *bag.*
    b. the *i* in *rib.*
    c. the *aw* in *saw.*
    d. the *eigh* in *sleigh.*
    e. the *a* in *was.*

33. An example of a vowel team syllable is

    a. *bone.*   **b.** *go.*   **c.** *stand.*   **d.** *diet.*   **e.** *herd.*

II. Multiple Choice. Select the word in each row in which the primary accent is correctly placed.

34. *sympathetic* **a.** *sym′pathetic* **b.** *sympa′thetic* **c.** *sympathet′ic* **d.** *sympathetic′*
35. *convulsion* **a.** *con′vulsion* **b.** *convul′sion* **c.** *convulsion′*
36. *geography* **a.** *ge′ography* **b.** *geog′raphy* **c.** *geogra′phy* **d.** *geography′*
37. *impeccable* **a.** *im′peccable* **b.** *impec′cable* **c.** *impecca′ble* **d.** *impeccable′*

III. Multiple Choice. Select the word in each row that is incorrectly syllabicated.

38. a. *ti ger* **b.** *pi lot* **c.** *ba con* **d.** *ca bin* **e.** *fe ver*
39. a. *win dow* **b.** *bot tle* **c.** *ham ster* **d.** *hat chet* **e.** *vic tim*
40. a. *merch ant* **b.** *ath lete* **c.** *e ther* **d.** *watch ful* **e.** *dis charge*
41. a. *re gion* **b.** *pi rate* **c.** *gi ant* **d.** *page ant* **e.** *as sas si nate*
42. a. *var i ous* **b.** *an i mal* **c.** *si mi lar* **d.** *av er age* **e.** *A mer i can*

IV. Multiple Choice. Select the words in each item (a, b, c) that contain a sound that the letter or group of letters at the left might represent. If none of the words contain a sound represented by the letter or group of letters, mark e. If all of the words contain a sound represented by the letter or group of letters, mark d.

43. *ti* **a.** *chin* **b.** *shop* **c.** *sure* **d.** All **e.** None
44. *ci* **a.** *shoot* **b.** *sit* **c.** *sugar* **d.** All **e.** None
45. *ge* **a.** *guest* **b.** *jet* **c.** *soldier* **d.** All **e.** None
46. *ce* **a.** *sign* **b.** *cat* **c.** *keep* **d.** All **e.** None

V. Multiple Choice. Select the word in each item (a, b, c) that contains the same sound as that represented by the underlined part of the word at the left. If none of the words contain that sound, mark e. If all of the words contain that sound, mark d.

47. *h̲orse* **a.** *honest* **b.** *who* **c.** *fight* **d.** All **e.** None
48. *m̲o̲o̲n* **a.** *grew* **b.** *blue* **c.** *do* **d.** All **e.** None
49. *w̲atch* **a.** *show* **b.** *whom* **c.** *one* **d.** All **e.** None
50. *si̲n̲g̲* **a.** *stranger* **b.** *bank* **c.** *get* **d.** All **e.** None

See page 207 for answers to Self-Evaluation: A Pretest.
Number correct _____

Part One

Phonics Self-Instruction

Chapter 1

Phonics and Literacy Development

When the word *phonics* is mentioned, many individuals visualize children grunting and groaning as they attempt to "sound out" unfamiliar written words. Some visualize children involved in time-wasting workbook activities and long hours of meaningless skill exercises. Unfortunately, too few educators today associate phonics with anything educationally positive. Yet strong data reveals that if phonics is correctly understood and applied in classrooms, it can play a very powerful role in the literacy development of children.

Are you aware of the strong research base revealing that phonics knowledge is causally related to successful reading and writing? Did you know that phonics knowledge is necessary for the development of sight word recognition, reading fluency, and even reading comprehension?

What are the phonics patterns, phonics elements, and literacy processes involving phonics that children can be taught to help them become better readers and writers? To help you answer this question, this book includes a pretest and a posttest. Do not look at the posttest now. You may even wish to remove it from the book and file it away until you complete your study of this text.

Turn to page 1 and take the pretest now. Correct it. At your next sitting, turn back to this section and continue reading.

Your success with this text will depend on two factors: first, your desire to learn about phonics, and second, your willingness to follow the directions as you proceed through the program.

This text is arranged in frames. In each frame you will be asked to provide missing information or make other types of responses. The left portion of the frame provides the answers. **It is essential that you write your responses before you see the correct answers.** To avoid looking at the left column while you read the text, cut the mask from the back cover of this book or use heavy paper to make one similar to it. Place the mask over the left-hand column to conceal the correct answers as you read the text.

When you have written your responses to the first frame, move the mask down to reveal the answers for that frame. Compare your answers with those provided. Since this is a teaching text (not a test) and is designed to guide you to the correct answers, you will more than likely find that you have responded correctly. However, even if your answers are wrong, you will learn something by following the instructions in the text. If you respond incorrectly, reread the frame and respond again. Equivalent answers should be considered correct, but make sure they are equivalent.

You will find much repetition and many opportunities for review. This will help you fix the important information in mind. At times it may seem that you are asked to make simple, obvious answers. You may be tempted not to write them and instead respond mentally or look at the answers while you are reading the frame. PLEASE DO NOT DO ANY OF THESE THINGS. IT IS ESSENTIAL THAT YOU WRITE YOUR RESPONSES BEFORE YOU LOOK AT THE ANSWERS!

It is also suggested that you not work too long at one sitting. Several short periods a day will produce better results than one long period.

You are now ready to begin the program.

expressive receptive	**1.** We use language so we can communicate with each other. In this communication process we either "send" messages or "receive" them. Therefore, language can be either expressive or receptive. When we speak, we express ourselves to others so we say that speech is an _____ process. When we listen, we are the recipients of someone else's speech so we call listening a _____ process.
sound sounds communicating	**2.** Speech, our primary language, is based on sounds. When we hear a spoken word, we associate the _____ we hear with something meaningful to us. Because word meanings are based on _____ , and because we learn to speak and listen before we learn to read and write, we say that the spoken language is our primary means of _____ with each other. (associating, communicating)
writing	**3.** We represent speech, our primary language, by _____ . We use a written language so we can communicate with people who cannot hear us speak—people who are not near us or people yet unborn.

spoken alphabet	**4.** The written language utilizes a system of symbols we call a code to represent the _____ language. In English, the code we use is composed of 26 alphabetic letters. We call the written code used to represent the spoken language the _____ code.
code phonics	**5.** An essential step in the reading process is called decoding. Decoding is translating the written _____ into spoken language. This decoding process can either be a fast process we call word recognition, or it can be a slower process we refer to as word identification. Both of these processes are founded on a knowledge of _____ . (phonics, word shape)
essential decoding	**6.** Although decoding is considered a "lower-order" process in reading and is not sufficient by itself for reading comprehension, it is nevertheless an _____ component of reading. Without _____ there would be no comprehension.
expressive receptive	**7.** In the written language, writing is a(n) _____ (expressive, receptive) process, whereas reading is a(n) _____ process. (expressive, receptive)
written receptive	**8.** Language can be classified as being either spoken and _____ , or expressive and _____ .
written letters (or symbols)	**9.** We study phonics so we can learn how the spoken language relates to the _____ language. *Phonics* is a term we use to describe the relationship that exists between the sounds of speech and the _____ used to represent those sounds.

Phonemes and Graphemes

three

graphemes

10. In our written language we use "smaller than syllable" word sounds called phonemes and represent them by graphemes (letters or letter combinations). For example, the word *man* has _____ phonemes. When we write
(How many?)
the word *man* we use the letters *m, a, n,* respectively, to represent its three phonemes. The letters used to represent phonemes are called _____ .

Phoneme

phoneme

sound

11. The *eme* suffix means "a structural element of language." The root *phon* means "sound." Therefore, the smallest sound unit in a word is called a _____ .
(phon + eme)
A phoneme is the smallest unit of _____ that distinguishes one word from another.

four

sound

phonemes

12. Say the words *last* and *fast.* Each word has _____
(How many?)
phonemes. The beginning phoneme in the word *last* and the beginning phoneme in the word *fast* are the smallest units of _____ distinguishing the words from each other.

Differences in word meanings are determined by _____ .

phonemes

phonemes

phonemes

13. Because only one phoneme can affect the meaning of a word, a word's unique sequence of_____ sets it apart from all other words (homophones excepted). Therefore, each spoken word in the language is recognized by its unique sequence of _____ .

Furthermore, the meanings we have attached to words are based on each word's unique sound—its coarticulated (blended) _____ .

phonemes writing	**14.** If we didn't have a written language, there would be little reason for our learning about phonemes since we speak and listen with little or no conscious awareness of phonemes. However, since we use letters to write words, and since those letters represent each word's _____ , an awareness of phonemes is very important for successful reading and _____ .
spoken phonemic awareness	**15.** In order for individuals to successfully learn to read and write, they must learn how _____ language maps onto written language. Phonemic awareness helps them grasp this concept. It is no surprise, therefore, to learn that the level of a child's _____ on entrance (vocabulary, phonemic awareness) to school is the best known predictor of his/her success in reading and writing.
grapheme graphemes	### Grapheme **16.** The *eme* suffix means "a structural element of language." The root *graph* means "drawn, written, recorded." Therefore, the _____ is the written (graph + eme) representation of the phoneme. Therefore, letters that represent phonemes are called _____ . A grapheme is the written representation of the phoneme.
phoneme grapheme phonics	**17.** In summary, then, the _____ is the smallest sound unit in the spoken language, and the _____ is the unit in the written system that represents the phoneme. The relationship that exists between graphemes and phonemes is called _____ . (phonics, reading) Phonics is a study of the relationship that exists between graphemes and phonemes.

graphemes (or letters) sound represented by the letter *p*	**18.** Technically speaking, we cannot write sounds (phonemes). Instead, we write _____ that represent sounds. When discussing the sound represented by a grapheme instead of the grapheme itself, I will use the symbol, / /. So when you see /p/ I am talking about the _____ (letter *p*, sound represented by the letter *p*). The symbol / / refers to the sound represented by a grapheme.

three   four
 	
three
 	
w
i
sh
	19. A grapheme and a letter are not the same thing. A grapheme always consists of at least one letter, but graphemes may also consist of more than one letter. In the word *wish* there are _____ phonemes and_____
	              (How many?) (How many?)
	letters. There are _____ graphemes in the word *wish*. The
	           (How many?)
	phoneme /w/ is represented by the grapheme _____ ,
	/i/ is represented by the grapheme _____ , and the
	phoneme /sh/ is represented by the grapheme _____ .

/th/ /n/ *th n*	**20.** Say the words *with* and *win*. The units of sound that differentiate these two words are _____ and _____ . The letters that represent these graphemes are _____ and _____ , respectively.
phonemes graphemes	**21.** In our language there are 44 separate sounds (or _____) used to create spoken words. These 44 separate sounds are represented by various _____ in written words.

26
 	
44
	22. In summary, then, there are _____ letters in our
	                          (How many?)
	alphabet that we use either separately or in combination with
	other letters to represent the _____ phonemes used in
	                          (How many?)
	our spoken language.

phonemes *ch*	**23.** Some of the alphabet letters are used with other letters to represent _____ . For example, the letters (graphemes, phonemes) _____ represent the phoneme /ch/ in such words as *chop, peach,* and *church.*
phoneme *a*	**24.** Some of the alphabet letters are used to represent more than one _____ . For example, the letter _____ represents three different phonemes in the following words: *can, cane, call.*
grapheme	**25.** Often, when a letter represents more than one phoneme, there are clues within the written word to indicate which sound the _____ represents. This text will help you (grapheme, phoneme) learn these clues so you can teach children to recognize and use them.
w *k* silent	**26.** Sometimes letters used in written words do not represent any sound. For example, in the word *sword,* the letter _____ does not represent a phoneme, and in the word *know,* the letter _____ does not represent a phoneme. Letters such as these are often referred to as _____ letters.

27. Although the phoneme/grapheme relationships existing between spoken and written words are not simple, once these relationships are properly understood, you will realize that phonics and spelling are not as inconsistent and unreliable as many people claim.

graphemes

We will begin our study with the consonant _____ , because the phonemes associated with these graphemes appear to be more consistent* than those associated with the

graphemes

vowel _____ .

*_Note:_ The sounds associated with the vowel letters are related to the written pattern of the syllable, so vowel letters appear to be more inconsistent than consonant letters. However, once an individual recognizes how the vowel sounds in written words are related to syllable patterns, consonant letters do not appear to be more consistent than vowel letters. Syllable patterns will be discussed in Chapter 3.

The reviews will give you important feedback regarding the effectiveness of your study. They will also help you determine whether you need to review the material presented in a particular section. Write your answers to the reviews on a separate sheet of paper. Correct your answers and analyze the results. After a few days, recheck yourself by answering the review questions again. Keep track of your scores so you will know where additional study and review are needed.

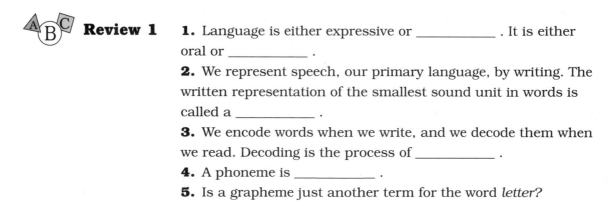

Review 1

1. Language is either expressive or _____ . It is either oral or _____ .

2. We represent speech, our primary language, by writing. The written representation of the smallest sound unit in words is called a _____ .

3. We encode words when we write, and we decode them when we read. Decoding is the process of _____ .

4. A phoneme is _____ .

5. Is a grapheme just another term for the word _letter?_

6. Practically speaking, American English words utilize (How many?) _____ phonemes.

7. How many phonemes are there in the word *athlete?*

8. How many graphemes are there in the word *athlete?*

Turn to the Answers section, page 203, and check your answers. You should have answered all of the questions correctly. If you succeeded, congratulations! If you did not succeed, review this section again.

Chapter 2

Consonants

Place the mask over the left-hand column. As you work through this section, it will be necessary for you to say some sounds out loud. Be sure that you are seated where this is possible. Remember, study the entire frame and write your responses before you look at the answers in the left-hand column.

vowels consonants *y* *w*	**1.** There are 26 letters in the alphabet. Five of these letters are called _____ and twenty-one are called _____ . Two of the letters used to represent consonant phonemes also represent vowel phonemes. These letters are ____ and ____ .
vowel	**2.** The letter *y* always represents a consonant phoneme when used to begin words or syllables; for example: *yellow, canyon.* When the letter *y* is not used to begin words or syllables, it represents a _____ phoneme.
consonant graphemes	**3.** The grapheme *w* always represents a consonant phoneme when used to begin words or syllables; for example: *water, reward.* In the words *highway* and *with*, the grapheme *w* represents a _____ phoneme because it is used to begin a syllable and a word. When the letter *w* is used with either an *a, e,* or *o* to form the vowel _____ *aw, ew,* or *ow* (*saw, few,* and *cow*), (phonemes, graphemes) *w* is a part of a vowel team. (Vowel teams are explained in Chapter 3.)

21	**4.** There are only _____ consonant letters, but there are (How many?) 25 consonant phonemes. Furthermore, 3 of the 21 consonant letters (*c*, *x*, and *q*) are superfluous, in a sense, because other letters of the alphabet represent the sounds those letters represent.

The Consonant Letter C

grapheme *k* *c* *s*	**5.** Say the phonemes in the word *cat*. The phoneme represented by the _____ *c* in the word *cat* is the same (phoneme, grapheme) phoneme represented by the grapheme _____ in the word *keep*. Say the phonemes in the word *cent*. The phoneme represented by the grapheme _____ in the word *cent* is the same phoneme represented by the grapheme _____ in the word *soap*.

c	**6.** Because the phonemes /k/ and /s/ are predictably represented by the consonant letters *k* and *s*, we say that the consonant letter _____ has no sound of its own.

The Consonant Letter X

grapheme *k* *s* /g/ /z/ *g* *z*	**7.** Say the phonemes in the word *box*. The phonemes represented by the _____ *x* in the word *box* are /k/ and (phoneme, grapheme) /s/ blended together. These sounds are the same sounds as those represented by the letters _____ and _____ in the word *books*. Say the phonemes in the word *exam*. The phonemes represented by the grapheme *x* are _____ and _____ blended together. These sounds are the same sounds as those represented by the letters _____ and _____ .

x	**8.** Because the phonemes represented by the grapheme *x* are represented by other consonant letters, we say that the consonant letter _____ has no sound of its own.

The Consonant Letter Q

9. The letter *q* does not occur in English words without a *u* after it: *quiet, queen, antique, opaque, quay.*

/k/ /w/ *k w* /k/ /k/ /w/	Say all of the phonemes in the word *quit.* The phonemes represented by the letters *qu* represent the phonemes _____ and _____ blended together. These phonemes are usually represented by the letters _____ and _____ . Sometimes the grapheme *qu* represents the phoneme _____ and at other times it represents the phonemes _____ and _____ blended together, but the letter *q* has no sound of its own.

18	**10.** When we subtract the 3 consonant letters that have no sounds of their own from the 21 consonant letters available, we have only _____ consonant letters that represent unique phonemes. Those consonant letters are *b, d, f, g, h, j, k, l, m, n, p, r, s, t, v, w, y* and *z.*

	11. The sounds predictably represented by these 18 consonant letters are listed here:
b	The consonant grapheme _____ represents /b/ as in **b**at.
d	The consonant grapheme _____ represents /d/ as in **d**og.
f	The consonant grapheme _____ represents /f/ as in **f**ish.
g	The consonant grapheme _____ represents /g/ as in **g**o.
h	The consonant grapheme _____ represents /h/ as in **h**ad.
j	The consonant grapheme _____ represents /j/ as in **j**ump.
k	The consonant grapheme _____ represents /k/ as in **k**iss.
l	The consonant grapheme _____ represents /l/ as in **l**amp.
m	The consonant grapheme _____ represents /m/ as in **m**an.
n	The consonant grapheme _____ represents /n/ as in **n**o.
p	The consonant grapheme _____ represents /p/ as in **p**an.
r	The consonant grapheme _____ represents /r/ as in **r**un.
s	The consonant grapheme _____ represents /s/ as in **s**un.
t	The consonant grapheme _____ represents /t/ as in **t**eeth.
v	The consonant grapheme _____ represents /v/ as in **v**oice.
w	The consonant grapheme _____ represents /w/ as in **w**atch.
y	The consonant grapheme _____ represents /y/ as in **y**es.
z	The consonant grapheme _____ represents /z/ as in **z**oo.
	12. If 18 consonant letters predictably represent 18 of the 25 consonant phonemes, there are graphemes for
7	_____ consonant phonemes that we have yet to discuss. (How many?)

	13. Six of the seven remaining consonant phonemes are represented by two-letter graphemes called consonant digraphs. The prefix *di* means "two," and the root *graph* means "written." Therefore a consonant digraph is a two-letter grapheme representing one phoneme.
ch	The consonant digraph _____ represents /ch/ as in **church.**
sh	The consonant digraph _____ represents /sh/ as in **sh**oe.
ng	The consonant digraph _____ represents /ng/ as in si**ng.**
th	The consonant digraph _____ represents /th/ as in **th**ing.
th	The consonant digraph _____ represents /<u>th</u>/ as in **th**e.
wh	The consonant digraph _____ represents /hw/ as in **wh**ite.
	14. The consonant phoneme we have yet to discuss is the /zh/ phoneme heard in such words as *divi**si**on* and *trea**s**ure*.
si	In the word *vision* the letters _____ represent the /zh/
s	phoneme, in the word *measure* the letter _____ represents the
z	/zh/ phoneme, and in the word *azure* the letter _____ represents the /zh/ phoneme.
25	**15.** In summary, then, there are _____ consonant
	(How many?)
18 (see frame 11)	phonemes. All of these phonemes except /zh/ are represented
5 (*sh, ch, ng, th, wh*)	by _____ single-letter graphemes and _____ two-
	(How many?) (How many?)
	letter graphemes; and one of those two-letter graphemes, the
th	_____ , represents two consonant phonemes, /th/ as in
	thing and /<u>th</u>/ as in **th**e.

graphemes graphemes 24 /zh/	**16.** When we refer to the "regular" consonant grapheme/phoneme relationships, we are referring to the phonemes associated with the 18 single-letter _____ presented in frame 11, and the phonemes associated with the 5 two-letter _____ presented in frame 13. These 23 graphemes represent _____ of our 25 consonant phonemes. The (How many?) consonant phoneme _____ is **not** predictably represented by any one grapheme.
/s/ /z/	**17.** Even though we use the word "regular" to describe the consonant grapheme/phoneme relationships discussed so far, many of the graphemes discussed also represent other phonemes. For example, in the word *rats,* the grapheme *s* represents the _____ phoneme, but in the word *dogs* it represents the _____ phoneme.
t *ed*	**18.** Furthermore, in some instances phonemes are represented by different graphemes than those expected. For example, in the word *fat,* the grapheme _____ represents the phoneme /t/, but in the word *wish**ed,*** the grapheme _____ represents that phoneme. We study phonics so we can understand when and why graphemes represent the phonemes they represent.

Review 2

1. Which two letters are used to represent both consonant and vowel phonemes?

2. The letters *y* and *w* always represent consonant phonemes when _____ .

3. Explain why the consonant letters *c, x,* and *q* are said to be superfluous.

4. There are 25 consonant phonemes used in spoken words. Eighteen of these phonemes are predictably represented by 18 of our 21 consonant letters (all of the consonant letters except *c*, *x*, and *q*). The /zh/ phoneme is represented by the graphemes *s*, *z*, and *si*. Write the 5 two-letter graphemes that represent the remaining six consonant phonemes.

5. A consonant digraph is _____ .

Turn to the Answers section, page 203, and check your answers. You should have answered all of the questions correctly. If you succeeded, congratulations! If you did not succeed, review this section again.

Consonant Phonemes

vocal	**1.** Consonant phonemes are produced by the speech organs: the lips, tongue, teeth, gums, roof of the mouth (also called the palate), and the _____ cords.
speech	**2.** Consonant phonemes are sometimes referred to as speech gestures because they are formed by moving those body parts used for producing _____ .
voiced	**3.** Some consonant phonemes, or gestures, are voiced and some are voiceless. When we produce consonant phonemes that are _____ , we vibrate our vocal cords. The vocal (voiceless, voiced) cords are comprised of two bands of elastic tissue that are positioned across the air pipe.

lips
 	
voiceless
 	
voiced
	4. Say the words *pat* and *bat*. Notice what your mouth is doing when you make the phonemes /p/ and /b/. Both phonemes are made by using the _____ . However, the consonant
	                    (teeth, lips)
	phoneme /p/ is _____ , while the consonant
	                    (voiceless, voiced)
	phoneme /b/ is _____ .
	                    (voiceless, voiced)
	Voiced consonant phonemes are produced by vibrating the vocal cords.

vocal cords voiceless voiced /b/	**5.** The only difference between the phonemes /p/ and /b/ is that one is formed by vibrating the _____ _____ , while the other is formed by blowing air through the lips. The phoneme /p/ is _____ , while the phoneme /b/ is _____ . Therefore, the phoneme /p/ is the voiceless equivalent of the voiced phoneme _____ .
identically voiced voiceless /f/	**6.** Say the words *fan* and *van*. Notice what your teeth and lips are doing as you say the beginning phoneme in both words. When saying the phonemes /f/ and /v/, the teeth and tongue are positioned _____ . However, the phoneme /v/ is (identically, differently) _____ , while the phoneme /f/ is _____ . The phoneme /v/ is the voiced equivalent of the voiceless phoneme _____ .
/z/ /s/	**7.** Say the words *zip* and *sip.* Notice that the phonemes /z/ and /s/ are both formed by placing your tongue near your gums and closing your mouth so your teeth almost touch. The phoneme _____ is the voiced equivalent of the voiceless phoneme _____ .
equivalent voiceless voiced	**8.** Say the words *tent* and *dent.* The phonemes /t/ and /d/ are _____ phonemes. However, the phoneme (equivalent, nonequivalent) /t/ is _____ , and the phoneme /d/ is _____ . (voiceless, voiced) (voiceless, voiced)
equivalent voiceless voiced	**9.** Say the words *gill* and *kill.* The phonemes /g/ and /k/ are _____ phonemes. However, the phoneme /k/ (equivalent, nonequivalent) is _____ , and the phoneme /g/ is_____ . (voiceless, voiced) (voiceless, voiced)

voiced voiceless	**10.** Say the words *that* and *thing.* The phoneme /<u>th</u>/ in the word *that* is _____ , while the phoneme /th/ in the word *thing* is _____ .
voiceless voiced	**11.** Say the words *ship* and *measure.* The phoneme /sh/ in the word *ship* is _____ , while the phoneme /zh/ in the word *measure* is _____ .
voiced voiceless voiceless voiced	**12.** Say the words *wait* and *white.* The phoneme /w/ in the word *wait* is _____ , while the phoneme /hw/ in the word *white* is _____ . Say the words *chump* and *jump.* The phoneme /ch/ in the word *chump* is _____ , while the phoneme /j/ in the word *jump* is _____ .

nine
 	
voiced
	13. There are _____ pairs of equivalent consonant
	        (How many?)
	phonemes. All of the _____ phonemes are produced
	       (voiceless, voiced)
	by vibrating our vocal cords.

/b/ /f/ /z/ /d/ /k/ /th/ /w/ /sh/ /ch/	**14.** The voiced equivalent for /p/ is _____ . The voiceless equivalent for /v/ is _____ . The voiced equivalent for /s/ is _____ . The voiced equivalent for /t/ is _____ . The voiceless equivalent for /g/ is _____ . The voiceless equivalent for /th/ is _____ . The voiced equivalent for /hw/ is _____ . The voiceless equivalent for /zh/ is _____ . The voiceless equivalent for /j/ is _____ .

/d/	**15.** Many of the voiced consonant phonemes are difficult to say in isolation. For example, when isolating the phonemes /b/, /v/, /g/, /w/, /r/, /l/, /j/, /y/ and _____ , we usually say buh, vuh, guh, wuh, and so on. The uh sound we add to these voiced consonants is like the /u/ sound you hear at the beginning of the word *up*.
/d/ . . . /i/ . . . /g/	**16.** We distort many of the voiced consonant phonemes when we try to sound out words, letter by letter. For example, we usually say /du/ . . . /i/ . . . /g/ when sounding out the word *dig*, instead of _____ . These isolated sounds when blended together are /du-ig/, which is a distorted version of /dig/. However, if consonant phonemes in the initial position of words and syllables are coarticulated with the vowels following them, this distortion is eliminated.
syllables vowel vowel	**17.** Consonant phonemes (and the graphemes that represent them) are used at the beginning and ending of words or _____ . (A syllable is the smallest part of a word (phrases, syllables) containing one _____ sound.) Consonant graphemes and phonemes are never used in the middle position of words or syllables. This position is reserved for _____ graphemes and phonemes.

beginning
 	
ending
ends
 	
begins
 	
pt
 	
syllables
	18. In the word *stretch,* the consonant phonemes represented by *str* are found at the _____ of the word, and the consonant phoneme represented by *tch* is found at the _____ of the word. In the word *accept,* the first *c* represents the phoneme /k/ which _____ the first
	                                    (begins, ends)
	syllable of the word, and the second *c* represents the phoneme /s/ which _____ the second syllable of the word. The
	           (begins, ends)
	consonant cluster _____ is used at the end the word *accept.*
	
	Consonant phonemes and graphemes are used at the beginning and ending of words or _____ .

 Review 3

1. Name the speech organs used for producing consonant phonemes.

2. Consonant phonemes are voiced and _____ .

3. Voiced consonant phonemes are produced by _____ .

4. When any two consonant phonemes are produced by the same speech organs, except one is voiced and the other is voiceless, they are said to be _____ phonemes.

5. Write the nine pairs of equivalent consonant phonemes. List the voiced phoneme in each pair first.

6. In syllables and single-syllable words containing three or more phonemes, there are, generally speaking, three phoneme positions. These positions are (a) initial, (b) medial, and (c) final. In which positions do we find the consonant phonemes and graphemes?

Turn to the Answers section, page 203, and check your answers. You should have answered all of the questions correctly. If you succeeded, congratulations! If you did not succeed, analyze your study procedure. Are you writing responses before you look at the answers? Are you summarizing to yourself what you have learned as you finish a page? Review this section again if you did not have a perfect score.

Single-Letter Consonant Graphemes (b, c, d, f, g)

phonemes graphemes letter	**1.** A study of phonics is a study of the relationships existing between graphemes and _____ . In this section of the book, we will study the phonemes represented by the 21 single-letter consonant _____ used in our written language. We will begin our study with the first five consonant graphemes of the alphabet: *b, c, d, t,* and *g.* Remember, a grapheme is not always a single _____ , like those we are studying first.
phoneme silent silent *m t*	**2.** The grapheme *b* predictably represents the _____ /b/ as in **b**at. Because of this consistent letter/sound relationship we say that the grapheme *b* is a "consistent" grapheme. Occasionally, *b* is _____ , meaning that it doesn't represent a phoneme. In the words *lamb, comb, debtor,* and *doubt,* the letter *b* is _____ . When *b* is silent, it either has an _____ before it or a _____ after it.
silent	**3.** In the words *climb, subtle, thumb,* and *bomb,* the letter *b* is _____ . The letter *b* is not often a silent letter. In the 5,000 most frequently used words of our language, only eight of them contain a silent *b*, and three of them have the same root (**climb, climbed, climbing**). *Note:* The 5,000 most frequently used words in our language comprise over 99% of the running words used in text materials written for use in the public schools.
/s/ /k/	**4.** The grapheme *c* has no sound of its own. However, it represents two different phonemes in written words. In the word *cinder,* *c* represents the phoneme _____ , and in the word *cat,* *c* represents the phoneme _____ .

/s/ e i y /k/	**5.** When *c* is followed by the vowels *e, i,* or *y,* it represents the phoneme _____ . In the words *cent, center, city, cider, cyclone,* and *bicycle, c* represents /s/ because it is followed by either an _____ , an _____ , or a _____ . When the grapheme *c* is followed by an *e, i,* or *y,* it represents the phoneme /s/. When the *c* is not followed by an *e, i,* or *y,* it represents the phoneme _____ .
/s/ an *e* follows *c* silent /k/ *c* is not followed by an *e, i,* or *y*	**6.** In the words *scene, fence, cellar, cement,* and *dance, c* represents the phoneme _____ because _____ . Notice that when the grapheme *ce* occurs at the end of words, the letter *e* is _____ . The letter *e* after the *c,* however, tells the reader that *c* represents the /s/ phoneme. In the words *climb, cat, cut, copy,* and *clock,* the *c* represents the phoneme _____ because _____ .
/sh/	**7.** In very rare situations, a *ce* in a multisyllabic word will represent the phoneme /sh/. In the word *ocean,* for example, the *ce* grapheme represents _____ . However, in the 5,000 most frequently used words in the language, only two such incidents are found: *ocean* and *oceans.*
/sh/	**8.** Occasionally, a *ci* in a multisyllabic word will also represent the phoneme /sh/. In the words *social* and *especially,* the *ci* grapheme represents _____ . However, in the 5,000 most frequently used words, only 12 such words were found: *official, officials, especially, ancient, social, precious, commercial, associated, sufficient, delicious, glaciers,* and *artificial.*

/k/ /s/	**9.** In the words *climb, crop, car, caterpillar, cupcake,* and *corn,* the *c* grapheme represents the phoneme _____ because it is not followed by an *e, i* or *y.* In the words *space, fancy, icy, scientist, cypress, cinnamon,* and *citizen,* the *c* grapheme represents _____ because, in each word, the *c* is followed by either an *e, i,* or *y.* About 76% of the time, the grapheme *c* represents the /k/ phoneme in words; about 23% of the time, it represents the /s/ phoneme; and about 1% of the time, it represents other phonemes.
/d/ phoneme	**10.** The grapheme *d* predictably represents the phoneme _____ as in **d**og. Occasionally the letter *d* occurs twice in a word such as in *add* and *odd,* and in these cases the grapheme *dd* represents the _____ /d/.
/j/ /d/	**11.** In very rare situations, the grapheme *d* represents the phoneme _____ as seen in the words *education* and *soldier.* However, 99% of the time, the grapheme *d* represents the phoneme _____ .
/f/ /f/	**12.** The grapheme *f* reliably represents the phoneme _____ as in **f**ish. Occasionally, the letter *f* occurs twice in a word such as in *off* and *stuff,* and in these cases the grapheme *ff* represents the phoneme _____ .
/v/	**13.** The grapheme *f* represents a phoneme other than /f/ in only one high-frequency word. That word is *of.* In the word *of, f* represents the voiced phoneme _____ .
/g/ /j/	**14.** The grapheme *g* represents the phoneme _____ in the word *go.* However, it also represents the phoneme _____ in such words as *giant* and *gentle.*

/j/ e i y	**15.** In the words *magic, gypsy, germ,* and *rage, g* represents the phoneme _____ . When the *g* represents /j/, it is followed by the vowels _____ , _____ or _____ . However, when the *g* is followed by an *e, i,* or *y,* it does not always represent /j/; sometimes it represents its own sound (*get, give, gynecologist*).
/g/	**16.** When the grapheme *g* is not followed by an *e, i,* or *y,* however, it generally represents its own sound (/g/). In the words *gun, got, gas,* and *glass, g* represents _____ because it is not followed by an *e, i,* or *y.*
e i y /j/ /j/	**17.** Most of the time, *g* represents /j/ when it is followed by the vowels _____ , ____, or _____ , and whenever *ge* occurs at the end of a word (*large, page, huge*), the letter *g* predictably represents the phoneme _____ . In these situations, however, the *e* is silent and is only used to tell the reader that the *g* represents the _____ phoneme.
guess ghost gnat dough night cough	*gnat guess ghost cough dough night* **18.** In the words above, *g* represents /g/ in the words _____ and _____ . The letter *g* is silent in the word _____ . The letters *gh* are silent in the words _____ and _____ , and the letters *gh* represent /f/ in the word _____ .
silent	**19.** When the letter *g* is followed by the letter *n* (*sign, gnaw, campaign, gnarl*), the letter *g* is _____ .
/g/	**20.** When words begin with *gu* followed by a vowel (*guitar, guard, guide*), *g* represents _____ and the letter *u* is silent.

h	**21.** When words begin with *gh* (*ghost, ghastly, ghetto*), *g* represents /g/ and the letter _____ is silent.
silent /f/	**22.** When the letters *gh* follow vowel letters (*caught, eight, sight*), *gh* is usually _____ . However, occasionally *gh* preceded by vowel letters (*rough, laugh*) represents the _____ phoneme. Even though *gh* represents /f/ occasionally when it follows vowel letters (5% of the time), 95% of the time, *gh* is silent when preceded by vowel letters.
/ng/ digraph	**23.** Remember that when the letters *ng* occur in words, they represent the consonant phoneme _____ that we hear in such words as *rang, long,* and *sing.* The *ng* grapheme is a two-letter consonant grapheme that we call a consonant _____ .
/g/ /j/ silent	**24.** Let's summarize what we know about the letter *g.* The letter *g* represents its regular phoneme _____ when it is not followed by an *e, i,* or *y.* When the letter *g* is followed by an *e, i,* or *y,* it usually represents the phoneme _____ , but not always. When *g* is followed by an *n,* it is usually _____ . The letter *g* represents /g/ in words about 70% of the time; it represents /j/ about 29% of the time, and it is silent less than 1% of the time.
/g/ beginning silent	**25.** Let's continue our summary about the letter *g.* The letter *g* represents its regular phoneme _____ when it is followed by a *u* plus a vowel letter (*guest*), and when it is followed by an *h* at the _____ of words (*ghost*). When vowel letters occur before *gh* (*naughty*), the *gh* is _____ .

g is not followed by an *e, i,* or *y*	**26.** The grapheme *g* represents /g/ in the word *glad* because _____. The grapheme *g* represents /j/ in the word *geology* because _____.
g is followed by an *e, i,* or *y*	
g is followed by an *n*	The letter *g* is silent in the word *gnome* because _____.
g is followed by a *u* and a vowel	The grapheme *g* represents /g/ in the word *guess* because _____.
gh follows vowels	The letters *gh* are silent in the word *midnight* because _____ , and the letter *g* in the word *ghastly* represents /g/, while the letter *h* is silent
gh begins the word	because _____.

Review 4

1. When we say that the letters *b, d,* and *f* are reliable graphemes, what do we mean?

2. Occasionally, the letter *b* is silent in words. When it is silent, it either has an _____ before it or a _____ after it.

3. State the generalization regarding when the letter *c* represents /s/ and when it represents /k/.

4. Most of the time, *c* represents the phoneme _____ .

5. When the letters *ce* or *ci* are followed by a vowel letter, *ce* and *ci* represent the phoneme _____ .

6. State the generalization regarding when the letter *g* represents its own sound and when it represents /j/.

7. Most of the time, *g* represents the phoneme _____ .

8. Ninety-five percent of the time the letters *gh* follow vowel letters, *gh* _____ .

9. When the letters *gh* begin a word, *gh* _____ .

10. Occasionally the letter *g* is followed by the letter *n*, and occasionally it is followed by a *u* and another vowel. When *g* is followed by the letter *n*, *g* _____ , and when *g* is followed by the letter *u* and another vowel, *g* _____ .

See the Answers section for the answers to Review 4.

Single-Letter Consonant Graphemes (h, j, k, l, m)

/h/ final silent	**1.** We continue our study of single-letter consonant graphemes with the second five consonant graphemes of the alphabet: *h, j, k, l,* and *m.* The grapheme *h* is quite consistent. It represents the phoneme _____ as in *had.* A distinctive characteristic of the letter *h* is that it never represents the _____ <div align="right">(initial, final)</div> phoneme in a word or a syllable. In other words, the letter *h* is seldom found at the end of words, and when it does appear (*oh, yeah*), it is always _____ .
no silent	**2.** Read the following words: *oh, hallelujah, ah, hurrah.* Do you hear /h/ at the end of these words? _____ <div align="right">(yes, no)</div> The letter *h* is _____ when it is found at the end of a word or syllable.
silent	**3.** Sometimes *h* is silent when it appears as the first letter of a word. There are no clues to help us know when, however. The letter *h* is always _____ in the words *heir, honest, honor, hour,* and their derivatives *heiress, honestly, honorable, hourly,* but there is some disagreement among individuals in different areas of the country regarding whether or not the *h* is silent in the words *herb, humble,* and *homage.*
k *r* *g* beginning	**4.** *H* is also silent when it follows certain consonants. Read the following words: *khaki, khan, rhyme, rhine.* The letter *h* is silent when it follows the consonants _____ and _____ . We have also learned that the letter *h* is silent when it follows the consonant _____ (*ghost, ghastly*) at the _____ of words. <div align="right">(beginning, ending)</div>

consistent or predictable /h/	**5.** The grapheme *h* is very _____ . In the 5,000 most frequently used words of the language, over 99% of the time, *h* represents the phoneme _____ , and less than 1% of the time, it is silent.
digraph *wi<u>th</u>, wi<u>sh</u>, <u>ph</u>one, <u>ch</u>arge, <u>th</u>at, <u>wh</u>ite*	**6.** Remember that a two-letter grapheme representing one consonant phoneme is called a consonant _____ . Most of the consonant digraphs contain the letter *h*, and should not be confused with the grapheme *h*. Underline the consonant digraphs in the following words: *with, wish, phone, charge, that, white*. (*Note:* A discussion of consonant digraphs follows this discussion of single-letter graphemes.)
/j/ final *dge* *ge*	**7.** The grapheme *j* is quite consistent. It represents the phoneme _____ as in *jump*. A distinctive characteristic of the letter *j* is that it never represents the _____ (initial, final) phoneme in a word. The graphemes that represent the /j/ phoneme at the end of words (*badge, huge*) are either _____ or _____. In other words, the grapheme *j* is used at the beginning of words (*joke*) or syllables (*enjoy*), but never at the end of words.
dge *ge*	**8.** When the phoneme /j/ is heard at the end of single-syllable words containing a short vowel sound (*edge, fudge, dodge, badge, bridge*), /j/ is generally represented by the grapheme _____ . Otherwise, the phoneme /j/ heard at the end of words (*large, huge, range, cabbage*) is represented by the grapheme _____ .
/y/	**9.** In the 5,000 most frequently used words of the language, the grapheme *j* represents the phoneme /j/ 100% of the time. In one low-frequency word, *hallelujah*, the grapheme *j* represents the phoneme _____ .

/k/ c *(cut, cat, coast)* /k/	**10.** Except when silent, the grapheme *k* consistently represents the phoneme _____ as in the word **k***iss*. Remember, the grapheme _____ also represents the phoneme /k/ when it is *not* followed by an *e, i,* or *y*. However, when you see the grapheme *k* in a word, you can be quite sure that it will represent the phoneme _____ .
/k/ an *e, i,* or *y*	**11.** Read the following words: *cup, cute, catch, cape, cost, coat, clock*. In all of these words, the grapheme *c* represents the phoneme _____ because the grapheme *c* is not followed by _____ .
k *i* or *e* Almost none	**12.** Since the grapheme *c* doesn't represent the phoneme /k/ when it is followed by the vowels *i* or *e*, the grapheme _____ is used to represent /k/ in these circumstances (*kitten, kite, kettle, kept*). In fact, most of the time the grapheme *k* is used in words, it is used to represent /k/ when /k/ is followed by the vowels _____ . How many words can you think of in which the grapheme *k* is followed by the vowels *a, o,* or *u?*
n	**13.** Study the following words to see if you can discover when the grapheme *k* is silent: *know, knife, knee, unknown, knocked, knot*. The *k* is silent at the beginning of a word or syllable when it is followed by _____ .
/k/ silent	**14.** The grapheme *k* is very consistent. It represents the phoneme _____ when used in written words, and it is _____ when it is followed by *n*. *Note:* In the 5,000 most frequently used words, the grapheme *k* represents /k/ 95.5% of the time it is used, and it is silent 0.5% of the time.

/l/	**15.** The consonant grapheme *l* is another very consistent grapheme. It represents the phoneme _____ as in the word *lamp.*
milk, held	**16.** Sometimes the letter *l* is silent. Study the following words: *talk, milk, folks, walk, yolk, could, held.* Underline the words in which the grapheme *l* is **not** silent.
no *silk, woud, chak* *gold, bel, shoud*	**17.** Sometimes *l* is silent when it precedes another consonant within a word or syllable. Is this a consistent pattern? _____ Rewrite the following words, omitting silent consonants. *silk* _____ *would* _____ *chalk* _____ *gold* _____ *bell* _____ *should* _____
very consistent /m/ /m/	**18.** Next we turn our attention to the grapheme *m.* This grapheme is _____ . *M* represents the phoneme (very consistent, not very consistent) _____ as in the word **m**an. When we see *m* in a word, we can be sure it represents _____ .

Ⓐ Ⓑ Ⓒ Review 5

1. What can you say about the reliability of the graphemes *h, j, k, l,* and *m*?

2. A distinctive characteristic of the letter *h* is that it never

_____.

3. On rare occasions, *h* is silent. This usually happens when *h* _____.

4. The grapheme *h* should not be confused with the consonant digraphs_____.

5. A distinctive characteristic of the letter *j* is that it never ____.

6. On rare occasions, *k* is silent. This usually happens when *k* _____.

7. Sometimes the letter *l* is silent. Although not consistent, the *l* is often silent when _____.

See the Answers section for the answers to Review 5.

Single-Letter Consonant Graphemes (n, p, q, r, s)

digraph /n/ /ng/	**1.** Our study of single-letter consonant graphemes continues with the third group: *n, p, q, r,* and *s.* The grapheme *n* should not be confused with the consonant _____ *ng.* The grapheme *n* represents _____ as in the word **n**o. The consonant digraph *ng* represents the phoneme _____ as in the word si**ng**.
/n/	**2.** The grapheme *n* consistently represents the phoneme _____ . Sometimes the letter *n* can be silent when followed by an *m* as in *autumn;* however, in the 5,000 most frequently used words of the language, this situation occurs only three times.
consonant grapheme	**3.** It might be interesting for you to know that the phoneme /n/ occurs more frequently in words than any other consonant phoneme. Therefore, the grapheme *n* occurs more frequently in words than any other _____ .
ng /n/ any other consonant grapheme	**4.** The most important things to remember about the grapheme *n* are: (a) it should not be confused with the consonant digraph _____ ; (b) it consistently represents the phoneme _____ ; and (c) it occurs in words more frequently than _____ .
/p/ digraph /f/	**5.** The grapheme *p* represents the phoneme _____ as in the word *pan.* It also is a very consistent grapheme. It should not be confused with the consonant _____ *ph* (**ph**one, *gra***ph**), which represents the phoneme _____ .

salm, sychology, tomaine neumonia, neumatic	**6.** The letter *p* is silent in words such as *psalm, psychology, ptomaine, pneumonia,* and *pneumatic*. However, these situations are rare and usually occur in low-frequency words. Rewrite the words above without the letter *p*. _____ _____ _____ _____ _____
beginning s t n	**7.** When the letter *p* is silent, it is found at the _____ of a word and is followed by the letters (ending, beginning) _____ , _____ , or _____ .
phoneme or sound u /k/ /k/ /w/	**8.** The letter *q* has no _____ of its own. *Q* does not occur in English words without the letter _____ after it (*mosquito, bouquet, quit, quake*). Sometimes the grapheme *qu* represents the phoneme _____ and sometimes it represents two phonemes blended together, _____ and _____ .
e last or final /k/	**9.** Study the following words: *opaque, mosque, plaque, antique, technique, unique*. Notice that the letter _____ follows *qu* in all of these words. Also notice that the *qu* plus the *e* represents the _____ phoneme of the word. The grapheme *que* in (What position?) these words represents the phoneme _____ .
first or initial /k/ /w/	**10.** Study the following words: *quietly, require, question, square, equal, quarter*. Notice that the *qu* in all of these words represents the _____ phonemes of words or syllables. (What position?) The grapheme *qu* in these words represents the phonemes _____ and _____ blended together.

/k/ /w/ /k/	**11.** Although there are a few exceptions, generally speaking, the grapheme *qu* represents the phonemes _____ and _____ when it is used at the beginning of words or syllables, and it represents the phoneme _____ at the end of words or syllables.
exceptions follow the pattern	**12.** Do the words *mosquito* and *conquer* follow the general pattern or are they exceptions? _____ Do the words *frequency* and *liquid* follow the pattern or are they exceptions? _____
/r/	**13.** The grapheme *r* is another very consistent consonant grapheme. It represents the phoneme _____ as in **r**un. It should not be confused with murmur diphthongs (*ir, er, ur, ar,* and *or*) which we will discuss in Chapter 3. Whenever you see a vowel before an *r* in a syllable, the *r* is a part of the vowel, and is called a murmur diphthong. A murmur diphthong is one grapheme, representing one phoneme, and should not be confused with the single-letter grapheme *r*.
beginning /r/	**14.** Study the following words: *right, read, bedroom, brick, already.* Notice that the *r* in these words is used at the _____ of words or syllables. When we see *r* at the (What position?) beginning of a word or syllable, we can be sure it represents _____ as in **r**un. The phoneme /r/ is the fifth most frequently used consonant phoneme in the English language.
/z/ /zh/ /sh/	**15.** The grapheme *s* represents the phoneme /s/ as in **s**un. However, this grapheme also represents other phonemes. In the word *was*, *s* represents _____ ; in the word *treasure*, *s* represents _____ ; and in the word **s**ugar, *s* represents _____ .

/s/ /z/ /zh/ /sh/	**16.** About 84% of the time, *s* represents the phoneme _____ as in **s**un. About 12% of the time, *s* represents the phoneme _____ as seen in the word *dog**s***, and about 4% of the time, *s* represents the phonemes _____ and _____ as seen in the words *mea**s**ure* and **s**ure.
digraph /sh/	**17.** The grapheme *s* should not be confused with the consonant _____ *sh* (**sh**oot, *wi**sh***), which consistently represents the phoneme _____ .
soon sun *has pans* *treasure leisure* *ensure sugar*	**18.** Study the following words: *ensure, soon, has, sun, sugar, treasure, pans, leisure.* The grapheme *s* represents /s/ in the words _____ and _____ . *S* represents /z/ in the words _____ and _____ . *S* represents /zh/ in the words _____ and _____ . *S* represents /sh/ in the words _____ and _____ .
/s/	**19.** In the initial position of words, *s* represents the phoneme _____ , except in the words *sure* and *sugar* and their derivatives. In the 5,000 most frequently used words, there are only three words (*sure, sugar,* and *surely*) in which *s* in the initial position does not represent /s/.
/z/ voiced /z/	**20.** In the final position of words, *s* represents the phonemes /s/ and _____ . See if you can determine when *s* represents /z/. Study the consonants before the *s* in each of these words: *jobs, birds, legs, hills, drums, plans, cars.* Are the consonants before the *s* in each of these words voiced or unvoiced? _____ What is the phoneme represented by *s* in these words? _____

unvoiced /s/	**21.** Study the consonants before *s* in each of these words: *topics, books, roofs, cups, boats.* Are the consonants before *s* in each of these words voiced or unvoiced? _____ What is the phoneme represented by *s* in these words? _____
/z/ /s/	**22.** When words end in *s*, and *s* follows voiced consonants, it represents the phoneme _____ . When words end in *s*, and *s* follows voiceless consonants, it represents the phoneme _____ .
/z/ /p/ /s/	**23.** When words end in *es* (*does, lives, poles, flies, tubes,* etc.) the *es* represents the phoneme _____ , unless the consonant phoneme before the *es* is /k/, /t/, or _____ (*techniques, makes, plates, pirates, ropes, shapes*). If words end in *es*, and *es* follows the graphemes *k, t,* or *p,* the *es* represents the phoneme _____ .

ⒶⒷⒸ **Review 6**

1. What can you say about the reliability of the graphemes *n, p,* and *r?*

2. An important thing to remember about the grapheme *n* is that it _____ than any other consonant phoneme.

3. The letter *n* should not be confused with the consonant digraph _____ , and the letter *p* should not be confused with the consonant digraph _____ .

4. On rare occasions, the letter *p* is silent. This happens when _____ .

5. The letter *r* consistently represents the consonant phoneme /r/ when it occurs _____ .

6. When vowel letters precede the letter *r,* the *r* is _____ .

7. The letter *q* never occurs in words without a _____ after it.

8. When *qu* is found at the beginning of words and syllables, it usually represents the blended phonemes _____ , and when *que* occurs at the end of words, it represents the phoneme _____ .

9. About 84% of the time, the grapheme *s* represents the phoneme _____ .

10. When the grapheme *s* occurs _____ , it represents both the /s/ and /z/ phonemes.

11. When the grapheme *s* at the end of a word follows voiced consonants, the *s* represents the phoneme _____ . Otherwise, it represents the phoneme _____ .

12. When the grapheme *es* at the end of a word follows vowels or voiced consonants, it represents the phoneme _____ . Otherwise, it represents the phoneme _____ .

See the Answers section for the answers to Review 6.

Single-Letter Consonant Graphemes (t, v, w, x, y, z)

/t/ /t/	**1.** In written words, the grapheme *t* represents the phoneme _____ as in **teeth** about 98% of the time it is used. Occasionally the letter *t* occurs twice in a word such as in **mitt** and **mutt,** and in these cases the grapheme *tt* also represents _____ .
digraph /th/ /<u>th</u>/	**2.** The grapheme *t* is very consistent. However, it should not be confused with the consonant _____ *th* (*with,* **that**), which represents the phonemes _____ and _____ .
/sh/ /un/ /ch/ /ch/	**3.** In multisyllabic words, we see *tion* frequently used (*ac**tion,** mo**tion,** solu**tion,** condi**tion***). When it is used, the letters *ti* most frequently represent the phoneme _____ and the letters *on* represent the coarticulated phonemes _____ . In very rare situations, the letters *ti* in *tion* represent the phoneme _____ (*men**ti**on, ques**ti**on*). When we see *tur* in multisyllabic words (*na**tur**al, cap**tur**e, mois**tur**e*), the grapheme *t* also represents the phoneme _____ .

silent	**4.** There are several common words that we have taken from the French (*debut, beret, bouquet*) in which the letter *t* is _____ . Occasionally, the letter *t* is also silent in some multisyllabic words such as *often, soften, listen, fasten,* and *moisten.* However, these situations are very rare.
/v/ *e* ends	**5.** The grapheme *v* consistently represents the phoneme _____ as in **v**oice. One of the most interesting things about the grapheme *v* (li**v**e, lea**v**e, lo**v**e, sol**v**e, twel**v**e, obser**v**e, ser**v**e, nati**v**e, cur**v**e) is that it is never found at the end of words without an _____ after it. In other words, the grapheme *v* never _____ a word. (ends, begins)
begins a word or syllable *o*	**6.** Earlier in this text you learned that the grapheme *w* predictably represents its consonant phoneme /w/ as in the word **w**atch when it _____ _____ . However, if the grapheme *w* follows the vowels *a, e,* or _____ , it is part of a vowel team (la**w**n, bl**ew**, t**ow**n).
/w/ syllables	**7.** Except when the letter *w* is silent in words (**w**rite, t**w**o, **w**ho), it consistently represents the phoneme _____ when it is used to begin words or _____ .
r	**8.** Analyze the following words: **w**rite, **w**rote, **w**rong, **w**riter, **w**rapped, **w**reck, **w**rist. We can predictably say that when the letter *w* precedes the letter _____ , the *w* is silent.

/ks/ /gz/ *taks egzist*	**9.** The grapheme *x* has no sound of its own. However, it does represent the coarticulated phonemes _____ in such words as *tax,* and the coarticulated phonemes _____ in such words as *exist*. If we were to write *tax* and *exist* using the letters usually associated with the sounds *x* represents in these words, we would write them _____ and _____ .
/z/ /eks/	**10.** Sometimes the letter *x* is used at the beginning of a word (*Xerox, xylophone, xenon*), and the phoneme represented by *x* is _____ . However, in the word *X-ray*, *x* represents the coarticulated phonemes _____ , which represent the pronunciation of its own name.
/ks/ /ks/ /gz/	**11.** Most of the time the grapheme *x* represents the coarticulated phonemes _____ as heard in the word *box*. In the 5,000 most frequently used words of the English language, the grapheme *x* is found in 95 words. In 82 of those words (86.3%), it represents the coarticulated phonemes _____ as in the word *mix*. In 11 words (11.6%), *x* represents the coarticulated phonemes _____ as heard in the word *exact*. In two words (*anxious* and *anxiously*), *xi* represents the coarticulated phonemes /ksh/ (2.1%).
begins words or syllables vowel	**12.** Earlier in this text you learned that the grapheme *y* predictably represents its consonant phoneme /y/ as in the word **y**es when it _____ _____ . However, if the grapheme is not used to begin words or syllables, it represents a _____ phoneme (*m**y**th, dr**y**, rh**y**me, cop**y***) or is part of a vowel phoneme (*pl**ay**, t**oy***).

yes, yellow, yet, year, lawyer *by, why, baby, happy* *say, boy*	**13.** Study the following words: **y**es, **y**ellow, law**y**er, **y**et, **y**ear, b**y**, d**ay**, wh**y**, s**ay**, b**oy**, bab**y**, happ**y**. Write all of the words in which *y* represents a consonant phoneme: _____ _____ Write all of the words in which *y* represents a vowel phoneme: _____ Write all of the words in which *y* is part of a vowel phoneme _____
vowel consonant	**14.** The grapheme *y* occurs more frequently in words as a _____ than as a _____ . (consonant, vowel) (consonant, vowel)
/z/	**15.** The grapheme *z* is consistently used to represent the phoneme _____ as in **z**oo. However, it may surprise you that the grapheme *s* represents /z/ more frequently in words than the grapheme *z*.
/z/ /s/ /zh/	**16.** The grapheme *z* is very reliable. In the 5,000 most frequently used words in the English language, *z* represents the phoneme _____ 100% of the time it occurs. However, in a few low-frequency words, *z* is used to represent the phoneme _____ as in the word wal**tz**, or the phoneme _____ as in the word sei**z**ure.

ⒶⒷⒸ Review 7   **1.** The grapheme *t* reliably represents the phoneme /t/. However, it should not be confused with the digraph _____ .
2. In words of more than one syllable, the *tion* suffix occurs frequently. It most often represents the phonemes _____ , but in rare situations represents the phonemes _____ .
3. On rare occasions, the letter *t* is _____ .
4. The grapheme *v* is (not very reliable, very reliable).

5. One of the most interesting things about the grapheme *v* is that _____ .

6. The grapheme *w* reliably represents /w/ when it occurs at the beginning of words and syllables, unless it is followed by the letter _____ . On these occasions, the *w* is silent.

7. The grapheme *w* is used to represent a vowel phoneme when _____ .

8. About 86% of the time, the grapheme *x* represents the phonemes _____ , and about 12% of the time, it represents the phonemes _____ .

9. The grapheme *y* reliably represents /y/ when it occurs at the beginning of words and syllables. It represents vowel phonemes when _____ .

10. The grapheme *z* reliably represents /z/, but in a few low-frequency words it represents the phonemes _____ and _____ .

11. The grapheme _____ represents the phoneme /z/ in more words than the grapheme *z*.

See the Answers section for the answers to Review 7.

Consonant Digraphs

digraph

ng

ing

/ng/

1. Earlier in this text you learned that a two-letter grapheme representing one phoneme is called a _____ . The consonant digraph in the word *sing* is _____ . This digraph occurs more frequently in words than any of the other consonant digraphs. It is found most often in the _____

(ang, ing)

inflectional ending of word variants. The *ng* digraph in *ing* consistently represents the phoneme _____ as in **sing.**

Note: A word variant contains a root word (*walk*) and an inflectional ending (*ed*): *walked.* Inflectional endings are used in word variants so we can communicate (a) present, past, or future tense (examples: *I walk to school every day. I walked to school yesterday. I will be walking to school tomorrow.*); (b) plurals (example: *girls*); (c) possession (example: *girl's*); (d) comparison (example: *smart, smarter, smartest*); and (e) first, second, or third person (examples: *I walk. You walk. She walks*).

longer

ng

2. The *ng* digraph also occurs in single-syllable words (*long, sang, rung, ring*) and other multisyllabic words (*finger, single, hungry*). Study the following words: *longer, ingest, engulf.* Only one of these words contains the *ng* digraph. Write that word: _____ . Sometimes we confuse multisyllabic words containing a prefix ending in *n* (*in, en*) and a root beginning with a *g* (*gest, gulf*) with words containing the _____ digraph.

/j/ /n/ /n/ *g* is followed by an *e*	**3.** There are other occasions in which *ng* occurs in words but doesn't represent a digraph. For example, when the letters *ng* are followed by an *e* or *i* (*cha**nge**, challe**nge**, ra**nge**, e**ngi**ne, cha**ngi**ng*), the *n* and *ge* or *gi* are usually separate graphemes, each representing separate phonemes. Do you remember what you learned regarding the letter *g* when it is followed by an *e, i,* or *y?* When the letter *e* or *i* is used after a *g* to indicate the phoneme _____ , the letter *n* represents its own phoneme _____ . Therefore, in the word *exchange*, the grapheme *n* represents the phoneme _____ , and the grapheme *g* represents the phoneme /j/ because _____ .

is
 	
is not
 	
/j/
	4. Vowel-beginning suffixes or inflectional endings (*er, est*) added to root words containing the digraph *ng* (*stro**ng** + er = stro**ng**er; you**ng** + est = you**ng**est*) should not be confused with root words ending with *nge* (*cha**nge**, challe**nge***). In the words *strongest* and *younger, ng* _____ a digraph even though
	                  (is, is not)
	there is an *e* after the *ng.* In the words *challenging* and *engineer, ng* _____ a digraph because the root words are
	      (is, is not)
	*challe**nge*** and *e**ngine**,* and the *ge* and *gi* in these words are used to tell the reader that *g* represents the phoneme _____ .

/ng/	**5.** Once you learn to recognize the *ng* digraph in words, you will also recognize that this digraph consistently represents the phoneme _____ as in *si**ng*** (almost 100% of the time it occurs in words).

/ng/	**6.** Study the following words: *congress, jungle, longer, angle.* The digraph *ng* in all of these words represents the phoneme _____ . The two syllables of the word *congress* written phonemically would be *kong. gres.*
	(*Note:* To write a word phonemically, we write, in the order in which they occur, the symbols that represent each phoneme in the word.
jung gul, long ger ang gul	Write each syllable in the words *jungle, longer,* and *angle* phonemically: _____ _____
/g/	Notice that the second syllable of each of these words begins with the phoneme _____ .
/g/ g	**7.** When the *ng* digraph occurs in multisyllabic words not ending in *ing* (*single, youngest, triangle, longest*), you can conclude that the syllable after /ng/ begins with the phoneme _____ (/gul/, /gest/, /gul/, /gest/) even though the written representation of the syllable does not contain the grapheme _____ (*sing.le, young.est, tri.ang.le, long.est*).
/th/ /th̲/ /th/ /th̲/	**8.** The second most frequently occurring consonant digraph in written words is *th.* This digraph consistently represents either the voiceless phoneme _____ as in **th***ing* or the voiced phoneme _____ as in **th***e.* About 59% of the time, *th* represents _____ , and about 41% of the time, it represents the phoneme _____ .

consonant letter	**9.** There is little to help you determine when *th* represents voiceless /th/ or voiced /th/. One pattern, however, does seem to emerge from a study of words containing *th*. Study the following words: *three, months, forth, threw, health, birth, depth, sixth, tenth, warmth, throne.* Whenever *th* is preceded by or follows a _____ in a single-syllable word, the *th* represents the voiceless phoneme /th/. An analysis of all the words containing *th* in the 5,000 most frequently used words reveals this to be a consistent pattern (100% of the time).
/ch/ /k/ /sh/	**10.** The next most frequently occurring consonant digraph found in written words is *ch*. This digraph represents the phoneme _____ as in ***church*** in most words (89%). In about 10% of the words in which *ch* is used, it represents the phoneme _____ as in *school,* **chemical,** **ch***aracter,* or *stoma**ch.*** In about 1% of the words, *ch* is used to represent the phoneme _____ as in *ma**ch**ine, ma**ch**inery, Mi**ch**igan,* or ***Ch**icago.*
peach, chase, porch *ache, orchestra,* *chorus, technical, echo,* *scheme* *machines*	**11.** Study the following words: *a**ch**e, pea**ch,** or**ch**estra, ma**ch**ines,* **ch***orus,* **ch***ase, te**ch**nical, por**ch,** e**ch**o,* and *s**ch**eme.* Write the words in which *ch* represents the /ch/ sound: _____ Write the words in which *ch* represents the /k/ sound: _____ . _____ . _____ . Write the word in which *ch* represents the /sh/ sound: _____ .

end
 	
short
 	
end
 	
is not
	12. Sometimes the phoneme /ch/ is written *tch*. Consider the following words: ca**tch**, ki**tch**en, ma**tch**, stre**tch**, wi**tch**, ske**tch**, di**tch**, scra**tch**. The grapheme *tch* occurs at the _____ of each word. The vowel sound in all of these (beginning, end)
	words is _____ . Consider the following words:
	      (long, short)
	pea**ch**, cou**ch**, ea**ch**, spee**ch**, coa**ch**, tea**ch**, rea**ch**. The grapheme *ch* occurs at the _____ of each word.
	      (beginning, end)
	The vowel sound in all of these words _____ short.
	      (is, is not)

end 100 short	**13.** Whenever the grapheme *tch* occurs in words, it is found at the _____ of words or syllables. It represents the phoneme /ch/ _____ % of the time. It follows _____ vowel phonemes. (long, short)
/sh/	**14.** The next most frequently occurring consonant digraph is *sh*, which represents the phoneme _____ as in **sh**oe. It consistently represents this phoneme.
/hw/ /h/	**15.** The digraph *wh* represents the phoneme _____ as in **wh**ite about 90% of the time. It represents the phoneme _____ as in **wh**o, **wh**ole, and **wh**om about 10% of the time.
/ng + k/	**16.** The letters *nk* at the end of words or syllables (thi**nk**, Tha**nk**sgiving, ba**nk**, mo**nk**ey, bla**nk**et) consistently represent (100% of the time) two phonemes blended together. Write those phonemes: _____ .

/ng/ /th/ /<u>th</u>/ /ch/ /k/ /sh/ /ch/ /sh/ /hw/ /h/ /ng/ /k/	**17.** In summary, there are six consonant digraphs that represent various phonemes. The grapheme _ng_ represents _____ as in si**ng.** The grapheme _th_ represents both _____ and _____ as in **th**ing and **th**e. The grapheme _ch_ represents _____ as in **ch**ur**ch** most of the time, but it also represents _____ as in e**ch**o and _____ as in ma**ch**ine occasionally. The grapheme _tch_ represents _____ as in wi**tch.** The grapheme _sh_ represents _____ as in **sh**oe. The grapheme _wh_ represents _____ as in **wh**ite, but it also represents _____ as in **wh**o occasionally. In addition, the letters _nk_ represent the phonemes _____ and _____ blended together as in sa**nk.**
_gh_ _f ph_ _f_	**18.** The consonant digraphs we have been discussing so far represent phonemes not generally represented by single-letter graphemes. However, there are two digraphs that represent phonemes that are generally represented by single-letter graphemes. The first one is _____ as in lau**gh.** This digraph represents the same phoneme that is most frequently represented by the grapheme _____ . The second one is _____ as in **ph**one. This digraph also represents the phoneme that is most frequently represented by the grapheme _____ .
100	**19.** The _gh_ digraph represents /f/ only when it follows vowel letters and even then it does it only 5% of the time. However, the _ph_ digraph consistently represents /f/ (_____ % of the time) when it occurs in written words.

tough, paragraph, phrase, telephone, elephant, photograph, telegraph

20. Say the following words: *mi**gh**t, hi**gh**, ei**gh**t, ou**gh**t, tou**gh***; *paragra**ph**, **ph**rase, tele**ph**one, ele**ph**ant, **ph**otogra**ph**, telegra**ph**.* Write all of the words containing a digraph that represents the phoneme /f/: _____

_____

_____

_____

Review 8

1. The consonant digraph _____ occurs more frequently in words than any other consonant digraph and is almost 100% reliable.

2. Describe those situations when readers think they see the *ng* digraph when they really don't.

3. About 59% of the time, the digraph *th* represents the phoneme _____ , and about 41% of the time, it represents the phoneme _____ .

4. Describe the situation in which the /*th*/ voiceless phoneme can be predicted in written words.

5. The consonant digraph *ch* represents /ch/ about 89% of the time. About 10% of the time, it represents the phoneme _____ , and about 1% of the time, it represents the phoneme _____ .

6. The consonant trigraph *tch* occurs at the _____ of words. It represents /ch/ _____ % of the time, and it follows _____ vowel phonemes.

7. What can you say about the reliability of the digraph *sh?*

8. What can you say about the reliability of the digraph *wh?*

9. The letters *nk* at the ends of words or syllables reliably represent the phonemes _____ .

See the Answers section for the answers to Review 8.

Consonant Blends

Eighteen	**1.** We have completed our discussion of the 25 consonant phonemes of the American English language. _____ of (How many?) these phonemes are predictably represented by single-letter graphemes. Six of the phonemes are predictably represented by
digraphs /zh/	the _____ *ng, th, ch, sh,* and *wh,* and one phoneme, _____ , is represented by various graphemes: *si* (*division*), *s* (*treasure*), and *z* (*azure*).
24 graphemes	**2.** Even though 23 graphemes (18 single-letter graphemes plus 5 digraphs) predictably represent _____ consonant phonemes (all of the consonant phonemes, excluding /zh/), you have also learned that some _____ (*rats, dogs*) occasionally represent more than one phoneme, and some phonemes are occasionally represented by more than one grapheme (*fat, phone*).
phonemes	**3.** Now that you have learned about the basic consonant grapheme–phoneme relationships, let's turn our attention to how some of the consonant graphemes are clustered in words. Consonant graphemes that are clustered with each other in written words represent consonant _____ that are blended together in spoken words.
s *g* consonant	**4.** Read the following words: **s***ag,* **st***ag.* Both words begin with the consonant grapheme _____ , and both words end with the consonant grapheme _____ . The *s* in the first word is followed by a vowel grapheme, but the *s* in the second word is followed by another _____ grapheme. When you say the second word, you blend the consonant phoneme /s/ with the consonant phoneme /t/ to get /st/, so we call *st* a *consonant blend.*

six *st, nd, cr,* *mp, sl, nt* ending	**5.** Study the consonant blends in the following words: ***stand,*** ***cramp, slant.*** In the words *stand, cramp,* and *slant,* there are _____ different consonant blends. In their order of (How many?) appearance those blends are _____ , _____ , _____ , _____ , _____ , and _____ . Consonant blends can occur at the beginning or the _____ of words or syllables.
one blended	**6.** Consonant blends should not be confused with consonant digraphs. Digraphs are two consonant letters representing _____ consonant phoneme, but blends are two or more (How many?) consonant letters representing phonemes that are _____ together.
str rap *trap* *strap*	**7.** Consider the word ***strap***. The consonant blend in this word is _____ . Since consonant blends are separate graphemes that are blended together, they can also be separated from each other without affecting the other phonemes in the word. For example, you can separate *st* from *r* in the word *strap,* and you have the word _____ . You can add *t* to *rap* and you have the word _____ . You can then add *s* to *trap* and you again have the word _____ .
sh /h/	**8.** Since consonant digraphs represent one phoneme, they cannot be separated. For example, in the word *show,* the digraph is _____ . If you separate the *s* from the *h* in the digraph *sh,* you no longer have a digraph. Once the *s* is removed from the *h,* you have two separate graphemes, *s* and *h,* that represent two different phonemes /s/ and _____ . Also notice that the word that is left in this situation (*how*) doesn't even sound like the word you started with (*show*).

stop, skip, slap *blue, plug, club, drop* *flag, snob, frog, glad*	**9.** Read the following words and underline those that contain consonant blends: stop skip shop slap this blue plug why club drop flag snob frog glad chip
thr *shr* *th* *r* *sh* *r*	**10.** The 27 beginning consonant blends that follow are arranged according to their frequency of use in American English words: *st, pr, tr, gr, pl, cl, cr, str, br, dr, sp, fl, fr, bl, sl, sw, sm, sc, thr, sk, gl, tw, scr, spr, sn, spl, shr.* Write the two consonant blends that contain digraphs: _____ . In the word *three*, the digraph _____ is blended with the single-letter grapheme _____ . In the word *shrub*, the digraph _____ is blended with the grapheme _____ .
nch *n* *ch* *nk* *ngth* *ng* *th*	**11.** The 15 ending consonant blends that follow are arranged according to their frequency of use in American English words: *nt, nd, ct, nce, nk, mp, lt, ft, nge, sk, pt, nch, nse, sp, ngth.* Write the consonant blend that contains one digraph: _____ . In the word *lunch*, the single-letter grapheme _____ is blended with the digraph _____ . Write the blend that represents the phoneme /ng/ blended with the phoneme /k/: _____ . In the word *sink*, *nk* represents the blended phonemes /ng/ and /k/. Write the blend that contains two digraphs blended together: _____ . In the word *length*, the digraph _____ is blended with the digraph _____ .

/k/ /w/

12. You learned earlier in the text that the letter *q* is always followed by the letter *u* in words. You also learned that *qu* at the beginning of words or syllables (*quiet, inquire, quickly*) usually represents the phonemes _____ and _____ blended together. When this happens, *qu* can also be considered a consonant blend. From the following words, write those in which *qu* is a consonant blend: *quake, unique, plaque, question, require, quit, equal, square* _____

_____

_____

*quake,
question, require,
quit, equal, square*

 Review 9

1. Explain the difference between consonant digraphs and consonant blends.

2. Sometimes a consonant digraph is blended with a consonant grapheme. Write a word containing a digraph blended with a consonant phoneme.

See the Answers section for the answers to Review 9.

Chapter 3

Vowels

Place the mask over the left-hand column. Write your responses in the right-hand column. Do not pull the mask down until you have written your responses to the entire frame. Make sure that you are seated where you can say sounds out loud. In order to get the full impact of this text, you must be able to say words and phonemes and listen carefully to what you say.

vowels	**1.** The 26 letters of the alphabet are divided into two categories: consonants and _____ .
44	**2.** These 26 letters are used either individually or in combination with other letters to represent the _____ phonemes that make up words.
Twenty-one 5 *a e i* *o u* no	**3.** _____ letters of the alphabet are used to represent the 25 consonant phonemes. Twenty-six letters minus 21 leaves only _____ letters. These letters are considered to be our vowel letters. Our vowel letters are _____ , _____ , _____ , _____ , and _____ . Are these the only letters that are used to represent the 19 vowel phonemes? _____ <div align="right">(yes, no)</div>

y	**4.** Say the following words: *myth, rhyme, my.* The letter used to represent the vowel phonemes in these words is _____ . The vowel phoneme in the word *myth* is the same vowel phoneme
it	heard in the word _____ . The vowel phoneme in the (*it, ice*) words *rhyme* and *my* is the same vowel phoneme heard in the
ice	word _____ . (*it, ice*)
i	When the letter *y* is used by itself in single-syllable words to represent a vowel phoneme, it represents the same phonemes the letter _____ represents.
e eve	**5.** Say the following words: *city, party, slowly.* The vowel phoneme represented by the letter *y* in the last syllable of these three words is the same phoneme represented by the letter _____ in the word _____ . (*eve, ice*) Say the following words: *deny, supply, decry.* The vowel phoneme represented by the letter *y* in the last syllable of these three words is the same phoneme represented by the letter
i ice	_____ in the word _____ . (*eve, ice*)
e *i*	**6.** When the letter *y* is used by itself at the end of multisyllabic words to represent a vowel phoneme, it represents either the same phoneme that the letter _____ represents in the word *eve* (*baby*) or the same phoneme that the letter _____ represents in the word *ice* (*deny*).

y digraph vowel	**7.** Say the following words: *h**ay**, th**ey**, b**oy**, b**uy**.* The vowel phonemes in these words are represented by the letter _____ plus another vowel letter. However, the two letters in each word represent only one sound. When two letters represent one sound, we have a _____ . Therefore, *ay, ey,* and *uy* are _____ digraphs. *Note:* The vowel team *oy* represents a special gliding vowel sound we call a **diphthong.** More will be said about that later.

a
ape
 	
oi
coin
 	
i
ice
 	
no
	8. The vowel phoneme in the words *hay* and *they* is the same vowel phoneme represented by the letter _____ in the word _____ . The vowel phoneme in the word *boy* is the
	   (ape, at)
	same vowel phoneme represented by the letters _____ in the word _____ . The vowel phoneme in the word *buy* is the
	   (gym, coin)
	same vowel phoneme represented by the letter _____ in the word _____ . Does the letter *y* represent any vowel
	    (ice, up)
	phoneme not represented by some other letter? _____
	                                                 (yes, no)

phoneme *i e* phonemes without	**9.** You have learned that *y* represents a vowel _____ , by itself, in words. However, when it does, it represents the same phonemes the letters _____ and _____ represent. You have also learned that when *a, e, o,* or *u* are combined with the letter *y* (*ay, ey, oy, uy*), these vowel combinations represent vowel _____ . However, the phonemes these vowel teams represent are also represented by other vowel letters. Because the letter *y* does not represent any vowel phoneme not represented by other letters, we could probably get along _____ it.

vowel does not	**10.** The letter *w* is also used to represent _____ phonemes. However, the letter *w* by itself _____ <div align="right">(does, does not)</div>represent a vowel phoneme.
w digraph	**11.** Say the following words: *few, law, show.* The vowel phonemes used in these words are represented by the letter _____ plus another vowel. However, the two letters in each word represent only one vowel phoneme, so *w* is a part of a vowel _____ .

few   use
law   fraud
show   oak
cow   out
 	
yes
	12. Match the words containing the same vowel phonemes: *few, law, show, cow, oak, fraud, use, out*
	
	    few _____
	    law _____
	    show _____
	    cow _____
	Do you think we could get along without using the letter *w* to represent vowel phonemes? _____
	<div align="right">(yes, no)</div>

vowel	**13.** Say the following words: *first, fern, fur, fork, far, hair, care, there, bear.* Notice that in each word you see the letter *r,* and you see at least one _____ letter before the *r.* Some people believe that the *r* does not represent a part of the vowel phoneme in these words. This is a serious mistake! When you see the following letter combinations in words, they represent vowel phonemes: *ir, er, ur, or, ar, air, are, eer, ear.* They are special vowel phonemes called *murmur diphthongs.*

does not	**14.** When the letter *r* begins words or syllables (**r**un, th**r**ee, **a**round, count**r**y), it _____ represent a vowel $\qquad\qquad$ (does, does not) phoneme. However, if the letter *r* is preceded by a vowel letter (or letters) the vowel letter/s and the *r* comprise a special vowel team that represents a vowel phoneme.
no	**15.** Are the vowel phonemes represented by murmur diphthongs represented by other vowel letters? _____ $\qquad\qquad\qquad\qquad\qquad$ (yes, no)
igh *i* *ice*	**16.** Say the words *h**igh**, l**igh**t, sl**igh**t, f**igh**t*. The vowel phoneme in these words is represented by the letters _____ . One could say that *gh* in these words is silent, which of course is true. It certainly does not represent any other sound. However, the *igh* grapheme pattern consistently represents the same vowel phoneme as the letter _____ in the word _____ . It will be shown shortly that vowel $\qquad\qquad$ (*it, ice*) phonemes can be predicted by letter and syllable patterns. Therefore, a good case could be made that *igh* represents a vowel phoneme.
no *y w r* *gh y*	**17.** The answer to the question "Are the vowel letters the only alphabetic letters used to represent the 19 vowel phonemes?" is _____ . In addition to the five vowel letters used to $\qquad$ (yes, no) represent vowel phonemes, the letters _____ , _____ , _____ , and _____ are also used. The letter _____ is used by itself to represent a vowel phoneme. However, it is also used with other vowels as a vowel digraph (*ay, ey, uy*), and it is used with the vowel *o* (*oy*) to represent a vowel diphthong. (A diphthong is a gliding vowel sound that we will discuss shortly.)

w	**18.** The letter _____ is used with the vowels *a* and *e* (*aw, ew*) to form vowel digraphs, and with the vowel *o* (*ow*) to form either a vowel digraph (*show*) or to represent a vowel diphthong phoneme (*cow*).
gh	**19.** The letters _____ are used with the letter *i* to represent the vowel phoneme heard in the word *ice*.
murmur diphthong	**20.** The letter *r* is used with the vowels preceding it (**bur**n, f**ir**st) to represent _____ _____ phonemes. Now that we have discussed the letters involved in the graphemes representing vowel phonemes, we next turn to the vowel phonemes themselves.

 Review 10 **1.** Besides the five vowel letters, what other letters are used to represent vowel phonemes?
2. When the letter *y* is used by itself in single-syllable words to represent a vowel phoneme, it represents _____ .
3. When the letter *y* is used by itself at the end of multisyllabic words to represent a vowel phoneme, it represents_____ .
4. Explain when the letter *r* is part of a vowel grapheme.

See the Answers section for the answers to Review 10.

Vowel Phonemes

voiced vowel	**1.** There are no voiceless vowel phonemes. All vowel phonemes are _____ ; we vibrate our vocal cords when producing all _____ phonemes.

a *a* *ai* *ay*	**2.** The 19 vowel phonemes, the graphemes representing them, and the key words used to refer to them are begun in this frame and continued in the next eight frames. *The vowel grapheme _____ represents /a/ as in **a**t *The vowel grapheme _____ also represents /ā/ as in **a**te or b**a** con. (The pattern of the syllable in which *a* occurs will help the reader know which phoneme it represents. More will be said about this shortly.) The phoneme /ā/ is also predictably represented by the vowel team patterns _____ (**ra**i**d**) and _____ (s**ay**).
e *ea* *e* *ee* *ea*	**3.** *The vowel grapheme _____ represents /e/ as in **e**dge. The phoneme /e/ is also represented by the vowel team _____ (br**ea**d). *The vowel grapheme _____ also represents /ē/ as in **e**ve or m**e.** (The pattern of the syllable in which *e* occurs will help the reader know which phoneme it represents.) The phoneme /ē/ is also predictably represented by the vowel team patterns _____ (f**ee**t) and _____ (**ea**t).
i *i* *y* *igh* pattern	**4.** *The vowel grapheme _____ represents /i/ as in **i**t. *The vowel grapheme _____ also represents /ī/ as in **i**ce and c**i** der. The phoneme /ī/ is also predictably represented by _____ (m**y** or rh**y**me) and the vowel team pattern _____ (n**igh**t). (Again, the _____ of the syllable or the vowel team in which *i* occurs will help the reader know which phoneme it represents.)

o *a* *aw* *au* *o* *oa ow*	**5.** *The vowel grapheme _____ represents /o/ as in *ox*. The phoneme /o/ is also predictably represented by _____ when it is preceded by a *w* (*water*) or followed by an *l* (*ball*). It is also predictably represented by the vowel teams _____ (*saw*) and _____ (*fraud*). *The vowel grapheme _____ also represents /ō/ as in *ode* and *so*. The phoneme /ō/ is also predictably represented by the vowel teams _____ (*soap*) and _____ (*show*). (The syllable and letter patterns will help the reader determine which phoneme is being represented.)
u *u* syllable *ew ue*	**6.** *The vowel grapheme _____ represents /u/ as in *up*. *The vowel grapheme _____ also represents /ū/ as in *use* or *u nite*. (The pattern of the _____ in which *u* occurs will help the reader know which phoneme it represents.) The phoneme /ū/ is also represented by the vowel teams _____ (*few*) and _____ (*cue*).
oo *u* *ew ue* *oo*	**7.** *The vowel grapheme _____ represents /ōō/ as in *moon*. The letter _____ in such words as *rude*, and the vowel teams _____ (*blew*) and _____ (*blue*) also represent /ōō/. *The vowel grapheme _____ also represents /oo/ as in *book*.
ow ou *oy oi*	**8.** *The vowel graphemes _____ and _____ represent /ou/ as in *cow* and *found*. *The vowel graphemes _____ and _____ represent /oi/ as in *boy* and *coin*.
ur ir er *ar* *or*	**9.** *The vowel graphemes _____ , _____ , and _____ represent /ûr/ as in *hurt*, *first*, *fern*. *The vowel grapheme _____ represents /ar/ as in *car*. *The vowel grapheme _____ represents /or/ as in *for*.

air are ere ear eer ear	**10.** * The vowel graphemes _____ , _____ , _____ , and _____ represent /âr/ as in **hair, care, there,** and **bear.** *The vowel graphemes _____ and _____ represent /êr/ as in **deer** and **year.**
geese reading badge fusion stretch	**11.** The symbols encased within the sound markers, //, in frames 2 through 10 identify the 19 vowel phonemes. An asterisk (*) is used whenever a new phoneme is introduced. The following words are written phonemically (according to their sounds). Spell each word correctly: gēs _____ rē ding _____ baj _____ fū zhun _____ strech _____
kum plēt dogz es tab lish rē sunt lē stâr	**12.** Using the symbols for consonant and vowel phonemes encased within the sound markers, //, write the following words phonemically: complete _____ dogs _____ establish _____ recently _____ stare _____
/ûr/	**13.** Write the symbol that represents the vowel sound in the word t**hir**st. _____
/o͞o/	**14.** Write the symbol that represents the vowel sound in the word cr**u**de. _____
/oo/	**15.** Write the symbol that represents the vowel sound in the word p**u**t. _____

/ā/	**16.** Write the symbol that represents the vowel sound in the word *br**ea**k.* _____
/ar/	**17.** Write the symbol that represents the vowel sound in the word *st**ar**t.* _____
/âr/	**18.** Write the symbol that represents the vowel sound in the word *st**are**.* _____
/ou/	**19.** Write the symbol that represents the vowel sound in the word *h**ow**.* _____
/oi/	**20.** Write the symbol that represents the vowel sound in the word *j**oi**nt.* _____
/ū/	**21.** Write the symbol that represents the vowel sound in the word *f**u**se.* _____
/o/	**22.** Write the symbol that represents the vowel sound in the word *h**o**p.* _____

/a/
/e/
/ē/
/ī/
	23. Write the symbols for the vowel sounds in the following words:
	    *str**a**p* _____
	    *n**e**xt* _____
	    *str**ee**t* _____
	    *m**y*** _____

24. Write the symbols for the vowel sounds in the following words:

/i/   *hymn*   _____

/ō/   *soap*   _____

/u/   *much*   _____

/or/   *stork*   _____

/êr/   *cheer*   _____

Review 11   **1.** There are voiceless and voiced consonant phonemes; however, there are no _____ vowel phonemes.

2. There are 19 vowel phonemes. Write the symbols for each vowel phoneme and give a word example for each.

See the Answers section for the answers to Review 11.

Long Vowel Phonemes and Graphemes

1. Long vowel phonemes are the sounds of the vowels' names. The long sound of the letter *a* is /ā/ as in *ate.* The long sound of the grapheme *e* is /ē/ as in _____ . The long sound of

eve

                                         (edge, eve)

ice

the grapheme *i* is /ī/ as in _____ . The long sound of the

                                     (ice, it)

open

grapheme *o* is /ō/ as in _____ , and the long sound of

                                   (open, odd)

use

the grapheme *u* is /ū/ as in _____ .

                                   (use, up)

2. We write a **macron** (—) over the vowel letter to indicate the long sound of the vowel. The macron is used to indicate that

name

the sound of the vowel is the same as the _____ of the vowel.

mane	**3.** The word element *macro* in the word *macron* means "long" or "great." If we were writing words phonemically, a macron would be placed over the *a* in the word _____ . (*man, mane*)
stāk *men chun* *sēk* *fūz* *bōn*	**4.** Write the following words phonemically: steak _____ men.tion _____ seek _____ fuse _____ bone _____
long *e* doesn't represent consonant	**5.** It was mentioned earlier that the pattern of the syllable indicates to the reader which phoneme a vowel grapheme is representing. Read the following words: **came, time, tone, use, eve.** The vowel phoneme in each word is _____ . Each (long, short) word ends with the letter _____ which _____ (represents, doesn't represent) a sound. The pattern of these single-syllable words is a VCe pattern. That is, the written syllable contains one vowel (V) grapheme, followed by one _____ (C) unit, followed by the letter *e*, which is silent.
long	**6.** Vowel graphemes in the VCe pattern generally represent _____ vowel phonemes. (long, short)
cape, wine, cope, *use, bathe, lathe*	**7.** Write the words containing long vowel sounds from the following list: *cap, cape, wine, win, cope, cop, us, use, bathe, bath, lathe.* _____ _____

yes	**8.** Do the words _bathe_, _blithe_, and _lathe_ fit the VCe pattern? _____ The grapheme _th_ in these words (yes, no)
one	represents _____ consonant unit/s. Therefore, the (C) (How many?)
digraph	consonant in the VCe pattern can be either a single consonant or a consonant _____ .
no	**9.** Are all vowel phonemes in VCe-patterned words long? _____ Although the pattern is quite consistent, (yes, no)
	there are vowels in VCe-patterned words that are not long. From the list of words that follows, write the words that do not contain a long vowel phoneme: _stone, come, these, some, fate,_
come, some, love	_love._ _____
e	**10.** Since the letter _v_ never ends a word without an _____ after it, you cannot use the VCe pattern with words ending in _ve_. Sometimes it works (_drive_), and sometimes it doesn't (_prove_), and sometimes it works in one context but not in another (_live_).
short	**11.** Words with consonant blends between the vowel and the silent _e_ (_pulse, rinse, fence_) are a VCCe pattern, and the vowel phonemes in these words are usually _____ . (long, short)
consonant long	**12.** We have discovered that when we see one vowel in a written syllable, followed by one _____ unit and a final _e_, the vowel grapheme is likely to represent its _____ sound.

long
 	
after
	13. There is another syllable pattern that suggests to the reader that the vowel grapheme represents its long sound. Read the following words: *so, go, me, he, ti ger, pi lot, ba con, la bor, mu sic,* and *hu mor.* The vowel grapheme in the first four words, and the first syllable of the last six words, represents a _____ vowel phoneme.
	             (short, long)
	Each syllable with the long vowel phoneme also ends _____ the vowel grapheme.
	  (after, before)

long	**14.** Written syllables ending in a single-letter vowel grapheme are called **open syllables.** The vowel sound represented by these graphemes is generally _____ . (short, long)
she, fro zen, **cra** zy, **mo** tel, **spi** der	**15.** Choose from the following list the words that contain open syllables: *com plete, she, suf fer, fro zen, cra zy, mo tel, spi der, cam el.* _____ _____
the VCe pattern (*rope*) and the open syllable pattern (*so*)	**16.** The syllable patterns suggesting that vowel graphemes represent long vowel phonemes are _____ _____ _____ _____ _____

sûr kus _jip sē_ _Frī dā_ _plāt_ _nō shun_	**17.** Write the following words phonemically: _cir cus_ _____ _gyp sy_ _____ _Fri day_ _____ _plate_ _____ _no tion_ _____
long the syllable pattern of _snake_ is VCe	**18.** The vowel grapheme _a_ in the word _snake_ represents the _____ vowel phoneme because _____ (long, short) _____ _____
long the syllable _fa_ in the word _favor_ is an open syllable	**19.** The vowel grapheme _a_ in the word _fa vor_ represents the _____ vowel phoneme because _____ (long, short) _____ _____
vowel	**20.** Open syllables (**ti** _ger,_ **ba** _con,_ **me, she, so**) end in single- letter _____ graphemes. (consonant, vowel)
gone, the, to, do	**21.** Although the VCe syllable pattern and open syllable pattern are quite consistent in predicting long vowel phonemes, there are, of course, unusual situations in which the vowels in these syllable patterns represent something other than the long sound. From the list of words that follows, write those words that contain vowels that represent something other than the predictable long sound: _gone, smile, the, to, strike, do, wide, shame, la dy._ _____

i	**22.** When *y* functions as a vowel in single-syllable words, it represents phonemes in the same way the letter _____ represents them. When the letter *y* is in an open syllable (*cr**y***,
i	*m**y***, *fl**y***), it represents the same sound the letter _____ represents in the open syllable (*m**i** ser, d**i** ver, f**i** nal*). When the
i	letter *y* is the vowel in the VCe pattern (*rh**y**me*), it represents the same sound the letter _____ represents in the VCe syllable (*t**i**me, b**i**ke, d**i**ce*).

Ⓐ︎Ⓑ︎Ⓒ︎ **Review 12** **1.** We write a _____ over vowel letters to indicate that they represent the long sound of the vowel.

2. The two syllable patterns that predict when single-letter vowel graphemes represent their long vowel sounds are

_____ .

3. Single-letter vowel graphemes in VCCe syllable patterns represent their _____ .

4. Since the letter *v* never ends a word without an _____ after it, you cannot use the VCe pattern with words ending in

_____ .

See the Answers section for the answers to Review 12.

Short Vowel Phonemes and Graphemes

	1. In this section we introduce the short vowel sounds and the syllable pattern that indicates when the single-letter vowel grapheme represents the short vowel phoneme.
	As you read the italicized words that follow, listen carefully to the vowel sound in each word and determine whether the vowel sound is long or short.
	In the word ***at*** the vowel grapheme *a* represents the
short	_____ vowel phoneme.
	(long, short)

short long	**2.** In the word **e**dge the vowel grapheme *e* represents the _____ vowel phoneme. In the word b**e** the vowel (long, short) grapheme *e* represents the _____ vowel phoneme. (long, short)
long short	**3.** In the word **i**ce the vowel grapheme *i* represents the _____ vowel phoneme. In the word **i**t the vowel (long, short) grapheme *i* represents the _____ vowel phoneme. (long, short)
short long	**4.** In the word **o**x the grapheme *o* represents the _____ (long, short) vowel phoneme. In the word s**o** the grapheme *o* represents the _____ vowel phoneme. (long, short)
long short	**5.** In the word **u**se the vowel grapheme *u* represents the _____ vowel phoneme. In the word **u**p the grapheme *u* (long, short) represents the _____ vowel phoneme. (long, short)
macron	**6.** In order to distinguish long vowel phonemes from short vowel phonemes, we place a _____ over the vowel graphemes representing the long vowel phonemes.

short long short	**7.** Some dictionaries place a diacritical mark called a **breve,** ˘, over vowel graphemes to indicate when they are representing short vowel phonemes.* In these situations, the short sound of *a* would be represented as /ă/. However, because English words contain more _____ vowel sounds than (long, short) _____ vowel sounds, most individuals now leave the (long, short) graphemes representing _____ vowel phonemes unmarked to save the cost and effort involved in marking them. *The linguistic relationship of "breve" to "short" can be observed in such words as *abbreviate* and *brevity*.
/a/	**8.** In this text all vowel graphemes representing short vowel phonemes will not have a breve over them. Therefore, the short sound of *a* will be represented as _____
catch, *desk, hunch, bath,* *sack, dog, up, add,* *pest* consonant consonant	**9.** Read the following words. Circle those with vowel graphemes representing short vowel phonemes: *catch desk lame hunch wine bath sack fake dog up rope so me add pest* All of the written words with vowel graphemes representing short vowel sounds end with _____ letters that (consonant, vowel) represent _____ phonemes. (consonant, vowel)
open	**10.** We call syllables ending in single-letter vowel graphemes (*so*) _____ syllables. We call syllables ending in consonant graphemes (*so**b***) closed syllables. *Note:* Both open and closed syllables contain only one single-letter vowel graphcme.

short long	**11.** The vowel phonemes represented by vowel graphemes in closed syllables are generally _____ . <div align="center">(long, short)</div>The vowel phonemes represented by vowel graphemes in open and VCe syllables are generally _____ . <div align="center">(long, short)</div>
gum, camp, tent, kiss, _yes, rock, bump_	**12.** Read the following words. Circle those words that are closed syllables: _gum camp zone tent kiss lo yes vice rock hope name bump say me_
consonant single- blend digraph single	**13.** Read the following closed syllable words: _u**p**, be**t**, be**st**, wi**sh**, lu**nch**._ Closed syllables do not need to begin with _____ graphemes (_up_). Closed syllables may end (vowel, consonant) with a _____ letter consonant grapheme (_be**t**_); they may end with a consonant _____ (_be**st**_); they may end with a consonant _____ (_wi**sh**_); or they may end with a consonant digraph blended with a _____ consonant (_lu**nch**_).
consonant short vowel murmur diphthongs are not	**14.** The phoneme heard at the end of closed syllables is a _____ phoneme, and the phoneme represented (vowel, consonant) by the single vowel is _____ . <div align="center">(long, short)</div>Consider the following words: _fir, her, hair, fur, for, far._ You learned earlier that vowels + _r_ represent _____ <div align="right">(consonant, vowel)</div>phonemes that are called _____ _____ . Therefore, since these words end in vowel phonemes rather than consonant phonemes, they _____ closed <div align="center">(are, are not)</div>syllable words.

closed	**15.** Syllables that end in consonant phonemes are called _____ syllables.
are not	**16.** Syllables that end in murmur diphthongs _____ (are, are not) closed syllables because murmur diphthongs represent vowel phonemes. Syllables with murmur diphthongs belong to the group of syllables called vowel team syllables. Vowel team syllables will be discussed later.
vowel team	**17.** The words *h**ur**t*, *f**ir**st*, *g**er**m*, and *f**or**k* are examples of _____ syllables. (open, closed, vowel team)
open	**18.** The first syllable in the words **pa** *per*, **ca** *ble*, **do** *nate*, and **ra** *cer* are examples of _____ (open, closed, vowel team) syllables.
closed	**19.** The first syllable in the words **win** *ter*, **sev** *en*, **mag** *ic*, and **nap** *kin* are examples of _____ (open, closed, vowel team) syllables.
pitch, gust, lid, tend, stump, slept, blond, stomp, brush	**20.** Read the following words and circle all closed syllable words: *pitch porch gust sharp page she lid tend squirt stump three slept blond starch slope stomp brush*

21. A phonogram is a sequence of letters (*ot*, for example) that can be seen over and over again in words: **c**ot, **d**ot, **g**ot, **h**ot, **j**ot, **l**ot, **n**ot, **p**ot, **r**ot, **t**ot, **bl**ot, **kn**ot, **pl**ot, **sh**ot, **tr**ot. There are six closed syllable phonograms that we call "foolers" because the vowel phoneme represented by the vowel letter is long rather than short. See if you can find the "foolers" and circle them.

ost	*ab*	*cab, crab, dab, jab, scab, stab*
	ost	*post, most, ghost, host*
	an	*can, fan, man, pan, ran, tan*
old	*old*	*bold, cold, told, sold, gold, hold*
oll	*oll*	*toll, roll, poll, stroll, troll*
olt	*olt*	*bolt, colt, jolt*
	ame	*came, game, lame, name, same, tame*
ind	*ind*	*bind, mind, hind, kind, find, grind*
ild	*ild*	*wild, mild, child*

22. You learned earlier that whenever *ge* occurs at the end of a word (*page, huge*), the letters *ge* predictably represent the

/j/   phoneme _____ . The *e* at the end of the syllable also helps the reader predict the vowel phoneme in the word. In such words as *rage, stage,* and *cage*, we have the VCe pattern,

long   suggesting that the vowel phoneme is _____ . However,

                                             (long, short)

in such words as *bridge, dodge,* and *edge*, we have the VCCe

short   pattern, suggesting that the vowel phoneme is _____ .

                                             (long, short)

is	**23.** The letter *d* in the *dge* grapheme _____ silent. (is, is not) Read the following words and listen carefully to the ending sound of each: *wage, fudge, sage, badge, age, smudge, huge, lodge, rage.* The ending consonant phoneme in all of these
is the same	words _____ , even though the spellings of (is different, is the same)
different	the consonant phoneme are _____ . The (the same, different)
/j/ short	consonant phoneme heard at the end of *smu**dge*** and *hu**ge*** is _____ . The vowel phoneme in the word *smu**dge*** is _____ , and the vowel phoneme in the word *h**u**ge* is (long, short)
long	_____ . (long, short)
	24. In words such as *badge* and *cage*, the *e* after the *g* is needed to indicate that the consonant phoneme at the end of the words is /j/. With the word *cage*, there is no problem in predicting the vowel phoneme because the syllable pattern is
VCe	_____ . However, with words like *badge*, there had to be some way to show that the vowel grapheme in the word represented the short vowel phoneme instead of the long one. Therefore, a *d* was placed before the *ge*, making the syllable
VCCe	pattern _____ . However, the *d* wasn't needed to represent a phoneme, so it isn't heard in the spoken word. Therefore, *dge* at the end of words represents the phoneme
/j/	_____ , as does the grapheme *ge*.

VCCe short /n/ /j/	**25.** Words such as *hinge, lunge, cringe,* and *plunge* reveal how words ending in *ge* are written to predict both the ending consonant phoneme and the vowel phoneme. These words represent a _____ pattern syllable, the vowel graphemes represent _____ vowel phonemes, the consonant *n* before the *ge* represents the phoneme _____ , and the grapheme *ge* represents the phoneme _____ .
ge /j/ murmur diphthongs /ûr/ /or/ /ar/	**26.** Read the following words: *verge, forge, large, merge, purge, surge, gorge.* These words all end with the same two letters, _____ . The ending consonant phoneme in all of these words is _____ . The vowels in all of these words are called _____ _____ . Therefore, these words belong to the vowel team syllable group. Write the symbol representing the vowel phoneme in the words *verge, merge, purge,* and *surge.* _____ . Write the symbol representing the vowel phoneme in the words *forge* and *gorge.* _____ . Write the symbol representing the vowel phoneme in the word *large.* _____ .
dge	**27.** The *dge* and *ge* word endings not only provide helpful clues for phoneme identification, but a knowledge of these endings can also help a person's spelling. When you hear the long vowel phoneme or a murmur diphthong phoneme in a word that ends in /j/, the spelling of /j/ is *ge.* When you hear the short vowel phoneme in a word ending in /j/, the spelling of /j/ is _____ .
i i sit	**28.** When *y* functions as a vowel in closed syllable words, it represents phonemes in the same way the letter _____ represents them. Consider the following words: *myth, hymn,* and *gym.* The phoneme represented by *y* in these closed syllables is the same phoneme represented by the letter _____ in the closed syllable _____ . <div align="center">(**sit**, **e**dge)</div>

syllable	**29.** You have learned that vowel phonemes can be predicted by the _____ pattern in which the vowel grapheme occurs. Vowel phonemes can also be predicted by certain letter patterns.
/o/ /o/	**30.** The consonant letters *w* and *l*, in the written language, seem to have a controlling effect on the vowel letter *a*. Read the following words: ***wa***ter, ***wa***nt, ***wa***tch, ***wa***sh, ***wa***nder, *sw****a****llow,* **al**so, *sm****a****ll,* c**all**, t**al**k, s**al**t, b**all**, *f****al****se*. The *wa* letter pattern in the first six words predicts that the vowel phoneme *a* will represent the phoneme _____ . The *al* letter pattern in words six through thirteen predicts the vowel phoneme *a* will represent the phoneme _____ .

 Review 13 **1.** Some dictionaries place a diacritical mark called a _____ over vowel letters to indicate they are representing short vowel phonemes.

2. American English words contain more _____ vowel
                                                                          (short, long)
phonemes than _____ vowel phonemes.
                          (short, long)

3. Which syllable pattern indicates that the single vowel in a word or syllable represents the short vowel phoneme?

4. Words ending in murmur diphthongs (are, are not) closed syllables.

5. Write the six "fooler" phonograms.

6. When *y* represents vowels in single-syllable words, it represents _____ .

See the Answers section for the answers to Review 13.

Vowel Teams

closed	**1.** We ended our study of the vowel phonemes that are predicted by vowels in open, VCe, _____ , and VCCe syllable patterns by introducing the concept that vowel phonemes can also be predicted by certain letter patterns.
vowel team /ā/	**2.** Some of the letter patterns that predictably represent vowel phonemes are called vowel teams. A vowel team is a vowel and another letter representing a vowel phoneme. The letters *ai* in the word **pai**nt are an example of a _____ _____ . The *ai* vowel team in the word *paint* represents the vowel phoneme _____ .
murmur diphthongs *or ir* teams	**3.** Vowel teams are found in vowel team syllables. You learned earlier that _____ _____ (examples: **por**ch, **bir**d) are found in the group of syllables called vowel team syllables. Therefore, the murmur diphthongs _____ and _____ in the words *porch* and *bird* are vowel _____ .
r diphthong	**Murmur Diphthongs** **4.** When vowel letters are followed by the letter _____ in a syllable, the vowel and the *r* represent a murmur _____ phoneme.
phoneme	**5.** A murmur diphthong grapheme is one grapheme representing one *r*-affected vowel _____ and should not be confused with the single-letter grapheme *r*.
herd, card, first, repair, burn, chair, fork, hear	**6.** From the following list, write the words that contain murmur diphthongs: *rustle, herd, card, rang, rainbow, first, repair, roast, burn, chair, fork, race, hear.* _____ _____

murmur diphthongs	**7.** The letter combinations *ir, er, ur, or, ar, air, eer, ear,* and *are* represent vowel phonemes and are called _____ _____ .
the same /ûr/ /ûr/ /ûr/	**8.** Read the following words aloud and listen carefully to the vowel sound in each word: *dirt, swirl, shirt, thirst, verb, herd, term, clerk, nurse, turn, curse, curl.* The vowel sound in each word is _____ . The vowel team *ir* (different, the same) represents the murmur diphthong phoneme _____ , the vowel team *er* represents the phoneme _____ , and the vowel team *ur* represents the phoneme _____ .
the same murmur diphthong phoneme	**9.** The vowel teams *ir, er,* and *ur* are called the /ûr/ triplets, because they represent _____ _____ .
/or/ the same the same	**10.** The vowel team *or* represents the phoneme _____ . Read the following words: *fork, storm, shore, tore, sport, horn, sore, store.* The *or* vowel team in all of these words represents _____ phoneme/s. Some of the (different, the same) words end in the letter *e,* but the vowel phoneme represented by the *or* vowel team is _____ in all words. (different, the same)
/ûr/ *w* /ûr/	**11.** Read the following words aloud and listen carefully to the vowel sound in each word: *word, work, world, worth, worry, worst, worms.* The vowel phoneme in each word is _____ . The letter before each *or* vowel team is _____ . We can say that this letter controls the *or* vowel team so that when it appears before the vowel team, the vowel phoneme it represents is _____ rather than /or/.

12. Read the following words aloud and listen carefully to the vowel phoneme in each word: *worked, short, worse, morn, worried, torn, workmen, cord.* Write the words in the proper columns below.

/or/	/ûr/
_____	_____
_____	_____
_____	_____
_____	_____

short   worked

morn   worse

torn   worried

cord   workmen

/or/

w

/ûr/

The *or* vowel team represents the phoneme _____ unless the letter _____ precedes it. When a *w* precedes the vowel team *or*, *or* represents the phoneme _____ .

/ar/

different

/ar/

/âr/

13. The vowel team *ar* represents the phoneme _____ *(sn**ar**l). Read the following words:* st**ar**ch, sh**ar**k, p**ar**k, y**ar**n, sh**ar**p, c**are**, sh**are**, b**are**, sp**are**, d**are**. The *ar* and *are* vowel teams in all of these words represent _____
                                   (different, the same)
phoneme/s. The *ar* vowel team represents the phoneme _____ , and the *are* vowel team represents the phoneme _____ .

/âr/

14. In the 5,000 most frequently used words, the *are* vowel team represents the phoneme _____ in every word in which it occurs, except the word *are.*

---

air

/âr/

15. Read the following words: h**air**, p**air**, ch**air**, f**air**, p**air**s, f**air**ly, rep**air**. The vowel team in these words is _____ . The *air* vowel team consistently represents the phoneme _____ .

---

are   air

16. The two vowel teams consistently representing the murmur diphthong phoneme /âr/ are _____ and _____ .

/ûr/ /âr/ /ar/	**17.** The *eer* vowel team consistently represents the gliding murmur diphthong phoneme /êr/ (*steer*). The *ear* vowel team represents that same murmur diphthong phoneme about 58% of the time, but it also represents the phoneme _____ (*earth*) 28% of the time, the phoneme _____ (*bear*) 12% of the time, and the phoneme _____ (*heart*) 2% of the time.
vowel team vowel /ou/ /oi/	**Vowel Diphthongs** **18.** You learned earlier in this text that vowel diphthongs are also found in syllables called _____ _____ syllables. A diphthong is a special gliding _____ sound. We will classify only two of our 18 vowel phonemes as diphthongs. They are both heard in the word *cowboy.* These phonemes are _____ and _____ .
/ou/ ou ow	**19.** Read and study the following words: *tr**ou**t, c**ou**ch, cl**ou**d, f**ou**nd, h**ou**se, sc**ou**t, br**ow**n, c**ow**, gr**ow**l, d**ow**n, cl**ow**n, fr**ow**n.* The vowel diphthong phoneme in all of these words is _____ . The vowel teams that represent the phoneme /ou/ are _____ and _____ .
/oi/ oy oi	**20.** Read and study the following words: *t**oy**, b**oy**, j**oy**, c**oy**, c**oi**n, v**oi**ce, **oi**l, n**oi**se.* The vowel diphthong phoneme in all of these words is _____ . The vowel teams that represent the phoneme /oi/ are _____ and _____ .
enjoy, *moist, destroy, joint,* *annoy, void, employ,* *groin, decoy, broil,* *loyal, spoil, voyage*	**21.** Read the following words and circle all those that contain the vowel diphthong /oi/: *enjoy loose moist moon destroy book joint* *annoy cool void employ loaves groin load* *decoy broil famous loyal brook spoil voyage*

crouch, *frown, mound,* *howl, drown, mouse,* *count, scowl*	**22.** Read the following words and circle all those that contain the vowel diphthong /ou/: crouch crook frown shrewd mound blew threw howl drown shoot mouse look count scowl
ou ow *oi oy*	**23.** There are two vowel teams that represent the diphthong phoneme /ou/. They are _____ and _____ . There are two vowel teams that represent the diphthong phoneme /oi/. They are _____ and _____ .
/oi/ /ou/	**24.** The vowel teams *oi* and *oy* consistently predict the vowel diphthong phoneme _____ . However, the vowel teams *ou* and *ow* are not as consistent in predicting the vowel diphthong phoneme _____ .

 down   *snow*
 gown   *blow*
 frown   *known*
 drown   *grown*
 town   *flown*
 howl   *blown*
 crown   *slow*
          show
	25. Read and study the following words: *snow, blow, down, gown, known, grown, frown, flown, drown, blown, town, howl, crown, slow, show.* Write all of the words that have the same vowel sound as *cow* underneath it. Write all of the words that have the same vowel sound as *glow* underneath it.
	
	     cow *glow*
	 _____ _____
	 _____ _____
	 _____ _____
	 _____ _____
	 _____ _____
	 _____ _____
	 _____ _____
	             _____

/ou/ /ō/	**26.** The vowel team *ow* represents both the vowel diphthong phoneme _____ as in *fowl*, and the long vowel phoneme _____ as in *so.* It represents the diphthong phoneme about 45% of the time, and the long vowel phoneme about 55% of the time.
/u/ /ō/ /o͞o/ /o/ /oo/ /or/ /ûr/	**27.** The vowel team *ou* represents the vowel diphthong phoneme /ou/ about 60% of the time. However, it represents the phoneme _____ as in the word *country* about 18% of the time. It represents the phoneme _____ as in the word *soul* about 10% of the time, and about 12% of the time, it represents other phonemes. It represents the phoneme _____ as in *group*, the phoneme _____ as in *sought*, and the phoneme _____ as in *should*. The grapheme *our* represents the murmur diphthong phoneme _____ as in *court*, or _____ as in *courage*.

two-
 	
one
	### Vowel Digraphs
	
	28. A vowel digraph is a _____ letter grapheme
	                (How many?)
	representing _____ phoneme. Vowel diphthong
	           (How many?)
	phonemes are gliding vowel sounds, and murmur diphthong phonemes are *r*-affected vowel sounds. The phonemes represented by vowel digraphs, however, are neither gliding nor *r*-affected.

teams trigraph	**29.** The following vowel _____ are called vowel digraphs: *ai, ay, ee, oa, ea, aw, au, ew, ue, oo, ie, ui, ey,* and *ei.* The vowel team *igh* is called a vowel _____ because three letters represent one phoneme.

a /ā/	**30.** The digraphs *ai, ay, ee,* and *oa* are the most reliable of all the vowel digraphs. They consistently represent predictable phonemes. The digraphs *ai* (**rain**, **saint**) and *ay* (**day play**) represent the same vowel phoneme represented by the letter _____ when it is in open and VCe syllables. Ninety-nine percent of the time, the digraph *ay* represents the phoneme _____ , and 96% of the time, the digraph *ai* represents that sound.
e	**31.** The digraph *ee* (**see**, **fee**t) consistently represents (99% of the time) the same vowel phoneme represented by the letter _____ when it is in open and VCe syllables.
o	**32.** The digraph *oa* (**boa**t, **soa**p) represents (95% of the time) the same vowel phoneme represented by the letter _____ when it is in open and VCe syllables.
sed, plad, sez, kē, ben, brod	**33.** Although the *ai, ay, ee,* and *oa* digraphs are very reliable, on rare occasions these digraphs represent phonemes other than those that would be predicted. Read the following words aloud and listen to the vowel phonemes in each word: **said**, p**lai**d, **say**s, qu**ay**, b**ee**n, br**oa**d. Using the phoneme symbols presented in this text, write each of these words phonemically. _____ _____

34. The digraph *ea* consistently represents one of two sounds, and there is no reliable way to determine which sound it will represent. Read the following words aloud: *weak, tease, sweat, dead, clean, bead, bread, head.* Write the words that have the same vowel sound as *speak* underneath it, and write the words that have the same vowel sound as *thread* underneath it.

speak	*thread*
_____	_____
_____	_____
_____	_____
_____	_____

weak   sweat
tease   dead
clean   bread
bead   head

---

35. The *ea* digraph represents the phoneme heard in the word *tea* most of the time. It represents the phoneme _____ about 74% of the time and the phoneme _____ about 25% of the time. In the words *great, steak, break,* and *yea,* the *ea* digraph represents the phoneme _____ .

/ē/

/e/

/ā/

---

36. The digraphs *aw* (*saw*) and *au* (*sauce*) consistently represent the phoneme _____ . On rare occasions, the *au* digraph represents the phoneme _____ as in *laugh.*

/o/

/a/

---

37. Read the following words aloud and listen carefully to the vowel sound in each: *pool, moon, shoot, good, wood, took.* The *oo* digraph represents _____ phonemes.
                    (How many?)
Write the words in which the digraph *oo* represents the /o͞o/ phoneme: _____

Write the words in which the digraph *oo* represents the /oo/ phoneme: _____

two

pool, moon, shoot

good, wood, took

/oo/ /u/ /or/	**38.** The digraph *oo* represents the phoneme /o͞o/ about 70% of the time it occurs in words. About 28% of the time, it represents the phoneme _____ , and in the words such as *blood* and *flood*, it represents the phoneme _____ . The *oor* vowel team in the words *door* and *floor* represents the murmur diphthong phoneme _____ .
/o͞o/ *fuel, few, cue, pew*	**39.** The digraphs *ew* (*new*) and *ue* (*due*) consistently represent the phoneme _____ . Sometimes these digraphs represent the consonant phoneme /y/ blended with the vowel phoneme /o͞o/. From the words that follow write those in which the digraphs *ew* and *ue* represent the phonemes /yo͞o/: *threw, due, fuel, few, cue, pew.* _____
/yo͞o/ /ō/	**40.** The digraph *ew* represents the phoneme /oo/ about 95% of the time it occurs in words. About 4.5% of the time, it represents the phonemes _____ as in *hew, mew,* and *fewer.* In the word *sew*, however, the digraph *ew* represents the phoneme _____ .
/o͞o/ /yo͞o/	**41.** The digraph *ue* represents the phoneme _____ about 94% of the time (*glue*). About 5% of the time, it represents the phonemes _____ as in *hue, fuel, value,* and *continue.*
u /k/ /w/ /k/	**42.** Readers need to be careful not to confuse the vowel digraph *ue* with the letters *que* in such words as *question, sequence, frequent,* and *unique.* The letter *q* does not appear in written words without the letter _____ after it. When *qu* begins words, the phonemes represented by that digraph are usually _____ and _____ blended together. When *que* is found at the end of words, it usually represents the phoneme _____ .

/ē/ /ī/ /e/	**43.** The remaining digraphs (*ie, ui, ey,* and *ei*) are fairly unreliable. The digraph *ie* (**pie**ce) represents the phoneme _____ about 65% of the time, it (**pie**) represents the phoneme _____ about 26% of the time, and it (**fri**end) represents the phoneme _____ about 9% of the time.
/o͞o/ /i/	**44.** The digraph *ui* (fr**ui**t) represents the phoneme _____ about 67% of the time, and it (b**ui**ld) represents the phoneme _____ about 33% of the time. Readers need to be careful, however, not to confuse the vowel digraph *ui* with the letters *qui* in such words as *quick, liquid,* and *equipment.*
/ē/ /ā/	**45.** The digraph *ey* (k**ey**) represents the phoneme _____ about 70% of the time, and it (th**ey**) represents the phoneme _____ about 30% of the time.
/ē/ /ā/	**46.** The digraph *ei* (s**ei**ze) represents the phoneme _____ about 39% of the time. It (v**ei**n) represents the phoneme _____ about 52% of the time (this percentage includes the *eigh* grapheme in such words as w**eigh**), and it represents other phonemes (h**ei**fer) about 9% of the time.

Ⓐ︎Ⓑ︎Ⓒ︎ **Review 14** **1.** A vowel team is _____.

2. When there is a vowel team in a syllable, that syllable is called_____.

3. When vowel letters are followed by the letter *r* in a syllable, the team of letters (the vowel/s and the *r*) is called a

_____.

4. When the letter *w* precedes an *or,* the *or* represents the phoneme _____.

5. A vowel diphthong is a gliding vowel sound. Write the four vowel diphthong graphemes and provide a sample word for each.

6. The vowel diphthong graphemes _____ and _____ reliably predict the vowel diphthong phonemes they represent, but the diphthong graphemes _____ and _____ are not so reliable.

7. The vowel team *ow* represents the _____ phoneme about 55% of the time and the _____ phoneme about 45% of the time.

8. How would you describe the reliability of the grapheme *ou* in predicting vowel phonemes?

9. A vowel digraph is _____.

10. The four most reliable digraphs (95–99%) are _____ .

11. The digraph *ea* represents the phoneme _____ about 74% of the time and the phoneme _____ about 25% of the time.

12. The digraphs *aw* and *au* reliably represent the phoneme

_____ .

13. The digraph *oo* represents the phoneme _____ about 70% of the time and the phoneme _____ about 28% of the time.

14. The *ew* and *ue* digraphs represent the phoneme _____ about 94–95% of the time and the phonemes _____ about 4.5–5% of the time.

15. How would you describe the reliability of the graphemes *ie, ui, ey,* and *ei?*

See the Answers section for the answers to Review 14.

A REVIEW OF PHONEMES AND THE GRAPHEMES MOST FREQUENTLY REPRESENTING THEM

There are 19 vowel phonemes represented by vowel graphemes. They are

/a/	**a**t	/e/	**e**dge, br**ea**d
/ā/	**a**te, r**ai**d, s**ay**, b**a** con	/ē/	**e**ve, f**ee**t, **ea**t, m**e**
/i/	**i**t, m**y**th	/o/	**o**ff, s**aw**, fr**au**d, b**a**ll
/ī/	**i**ce, c**i** der, h**igh**, m**y**	/ō/	s**o**, **oa**k, **o**de, sh**ow**
/u/	**u**p	/oo/	b**oo**k, p**u**t
/ū/	**u**se, f**ew**, c**ue**, **u** nite	/o͞o/	m**oo**n, r**u**de, bl**ue**, gr**ew**
/ûr/	b**ir**d, f**ur**, f**er**n	/ar/	c**ar**
/or/	f**or**	/oi/	b**oy**, **oi**l
/ou/	c**ow**, f**ou**nd	/âr/	h**air**, c**are**, th**ere**, b**ear**
		/êr/	d**ee**r, y**ear**

There are 25 consonant phonemes represented by the following graphemes:

/b/	**b**at	/d/	**d**og
/f/	**f**ish	/g/	**g**o
/h/	**h**ad	/j/	**j**ump, **g**em, ra**ge**, fu**dge**
/k/	**k**iss, **c**at, ki**ck**	/l/	**l**amp
/m/	**m**an	/n/	**n**o
/p/	**p**an	/r/	**r**un
/s/	**s**un, **c**ent, gee**se**	/t/	**t**eeth
/v/	**v**oice	/w/	**w**atch
/y/	**y**es	/z/	**z**oo, dog**s**, ro**se**
/sh/	**sh**oe	/ch/	**ch**urch
/th/	**th**e	/th/	**th**ing
/ng/	si**ng**	/zh/	mea**s**ure
/hw/	**wh**ite		

Chapter 4

Syllabication and Accent

Remember to place the mask over the left-hand column. Write your responses in the right-hand column before you pull the mask down.

The Syllable

vowel sound	**1.** A syllable is the smallest part of a word containing one _____ . It is the smallest pronunciation unit in the language.
	The syllable is the smallest unit of pronunciation.
vowel syllables	**2.** Since each syllable contains only one _____ phoneme, the number of vowel phonemes you hear in a word equals the number of _____ in that word.
voiced	**3.** All vowel phonemes are _____ phonemes. (voiceless, voiced) Therefore, if you touch the part of your throat containing the vocal cords, you can feel the vibration of the vocal cords as you say the syllables of a word. *Note:* Consonant phonemes, voiced or voiceless, are coarticulated with vowel phonemes, so we can't detect them as easily as we can vowel phonemes.

	4. Place your hand against your larynx (the larynx is the structure at the upper end of the trachea, containing the vocal cords). Read the following words aloud and write the number of vibrations you feel as you say the words.
3 2 1 3 1 2	_____ *yesterday* _____ *complete* _____ *seed* _____ *obsolete* _____ *fair* _____ *sofa*
feel	**5.** If you can hear the vowel sounds in words, you can determine the number of syllables they contain. However, if you can't hear vowel sounds, you can _____ them by saying the words aloud while your hand is against your larynx.
phoneme 1 2	**6.** A syllable may have more than one vowel letter but only one vowel _____ . How many syllables are in the word *kissed?* _____ How many vowel letters are in the word *kissed?* _____ .
	### *Onsets and Rimes*
rime onset	**7.** Although the syllable is acoustically an unanalyzable spoken unit, many reading educators analyze syllables psychologically in terms of onsets and rimes. The syllable's _____ is the rhyming component in the syllable (*m**ap**,* (onset, rime) *tr**ap***), and the _____ is the component before the (onset, rime) rhyming component (***m***ap, ***tr***ap).

onset
 	
rime
	8. In the single-syllable word *jump*, the grapheme *j* is the syllable's _____ , and the graphemes *ump* comprise
	                (onset, rime)
	the syllable's _____ .
	                (onset, rime)

phonemes	**9.** Many educators emphasize onsets and rimes as they seek to help young children develop phonemic awareness, since a phonological awareness of rhymes precedes an awareness of _____ . (syllables, phonemes)
rhyming alliteration	**10.** Children phonologically perceive rhyming components of words even before they perceive the consonant sounds preceding them. Therefore, _____ books are (rhyming, alliteration) more relevant to preschool children than books stressing _____ . (rhyming, alliteration)
rime onset	**11.** Since young children find it easier to perceive the _____ in a syllable before perceiving its (onset, rime) _____ , many first grade teachers begin their phonics (onset, rime) instruction using phonograms. In this manner they help children develop some phonics knowledge while they are also developing phonemic awareness.
ock	**12.** A phonogram is another name for rime. The phonogram, or rime, _____ is found in all of the following words: **s*ock*, bl*ock*, r*ock*, d*ock*, sm*ock*, l*ock*,** and **m*ock*.**
phonemes	**13.** Young children find it easier to separate or combine onsets from rimes than to separate either onsets and rimes into separate _____ . Therefore, many teachers have found phonograms to be a useful tool to help young children become aware of onsets—an important key for the development of higher levels of phonemic awareness.

cop, hop, mop, pop, top	**14.** As teachers help children become aware of initial consonant phonemes (onsets) by studying rimes and onsets, they also help them become aware of the graphemes that represent the onsets. For example, write five words by combining each of the five onsets *c, h, m, p,* and *t* to the *op* phonogram: _____ _____
phonemes	**15.** As children grow in phonemic awareness and phonics knowledge, they need to move beyond onsets and rimes so they can learn how all speech sounds, or _____ , are represented by graphemes, or letters of the alphabet.
graphemes phonemes	### Why Study Syllables? **16.** Before we discuss syllables in more detail, let's talk about why reading teachers are concerned about syllabication. Phonics is a study of the relationship between the _____ in written words and the _____ in spoken words.
syllable	**17.** A study of phonics involves a study of _____ patterns because the pattern of the written syllable suggests to the reader which phoneme the vowel grapheme is representing.
long short	**18.** Vowel graphemes in open syllables (*so, me, spi der, pa per, bu gle*) generally represent _____ vowel (short, long) phonemes. Vowel graphemes in closed syllables (*got, met, spin, past, bug*) generally represent _____ vowel (short, long) phonemes.

fi	**19.** When young students are faced with words of more than one syllable, these syllable patterns are not easily identified. In the words *fatal* and *fiber,* young children may focus their attention on familiar letter sequences within the words such as *fat* and *fib,* if they can't identify the *fa* and _____ syllable patterns in the words.
phonics	**20.** We study syllabication so we can help young readers find the appropriate syllable patterns in multisyllabic words so they can use their _____ knowledge to identify them. As we continue our discussion of syllabication, keep this goal in mind.

Accented and Unaccented Syllables and the Schwa Phoneme

syllable	**21.** When we pronounce words of more than one syllable, we accent (emphasize) some syllables more than others. We show this emphasis or stress by placing an accent mark (ʹ) at the end of the accented _____ . The vowels in syllables that are not accented often represent a phoneme that we call the schwa.

two	**22.** In the word *sofa* there are _____ syllables because (How many?) the word contains two vowel phonemes. The vowel phoneme in
accented	the first syllable (*so'*) is _____ , and the (accented, unaccented)
/ō/ unaccented	sound of the phoneme is _____ . The vowel phoneme in the second syllable (*fa*) is _____ , and the (accented, unaccented)
/u/ up	sound of the phoneme is _____ . It is the same phoneme we hear at the beginning of the word _____ . It is called (*up, use*) the *schwa phoneme*.
unaccented	**23.** The schwa phoneme is the phoneme that is generally used in _____ syllables. When we accent or (accented, unaccented) emphasize syllables, the schwa phoneme is not used.
first second first second	**24.** In the word *pi' lot,* the _____ syllable is accented, (first, second) and the _____ syllable is unaccented. The vowel in the (first, second) _____ syllable represents its long sound and the vowel in the _____ syllable represents the schwa sound.
second first first second	**25.** In the word *a lone'* the _____ syllable is accented, (first, second) and the _____ syllable is unaccented. The vowel in the (first, second) _____ syllable represents the schwa sound, and the vowel in the _____ syllable represents its long sound.

26. In words of more than one syllable, more than one syllable may be stressed. Read the following words aloud. Listen carefully for the schwa phoneme in each word. Write the syllables in each word phonemically, using the phonemic symbols presented in the text, and indicate which syllable (first, second, third) contains the schwa phoneme:

Word		Syllable Containing Schwa
complain	_____	_____
barbecue	_____	_____
navigate	_____	_____
melon	_____	_____
plasma	_____	_____
complete	_____	_____

kum plān'   1
bar' bu kyoō,   2
nav' u gāt'   2
mel' un   2
plaz' mu   2
kum plēt'   1

27. The schwa phoneme is not found in all multisyllabic words. Circle the multisyllabic words below that do not contain the schwa.

panic   button   intrust   animal   never

panic   intrust never

28. <u>Open Syllable</u>   <u>Closed Syllable</u>   <u>Vowel Team Syllable</u>

Open Syllable	Closed Syllable	Vowel Team Syllable
fe' ver	*rob' in*	*dai' ly*
go' pher	*pen' cil*	*loy' al*
a go'	*con struct'*	*com plain'*

Vowel graphemes in accented syllables represent the vowel phonemes suggested by the _____ pattern in which they occur, or they represent the phonemes suggested by the vowel team pattern in the vowel team syllable.

syllable

29. Vowel graphemes in unaccented syllables often represent the _____ phoneme. Vowel graphemes in unaccented syllables do not represent the schwa if the unaccented syllable (*tim' **ber***) ends in a _____ _____ , or the letter _____ (*hap' py*).

schwa

murmur diphthong

y

/ī/ /ē/	**30.** Read the following words and listen carefully to the vowel phoneme the grapheme *y* represents in accented and unaccented syllables: *de ny′, ap ply′, ba′ by, par′ ty.* The grapheme *y* represents the phoneme _____ in accented syllables, and the phoneme _____ in unaccented syllables.
accent schwa	**31.** When attempting to decode multisyllabic words not recognized by sight, it is often helpful to have some idea where to place the _____ on a syllable and when to try the _____ phoneme. Some clues exist regarding where the accent may be found in words.

Accent Placement Clues

accented	**1.** All single-syllable words are considered to be _____ even though dictionaries do not place (accented, unaccented) accent marks on them.
root word affixes	**2.** Prefixes (**a**live) and suffixes (hate**ful**) are often separate syllables. When a word contains affixes, the _____ (affixes, root word) are/is more likely to receive the accent than the _____ . (affixes, root word)
first	**3.** In compound words (*homework, fireman*), the accent usually falls on or within the _____ word. (first, second)

first second	**4.** In words that are used as both nouns and verbs (*object*, *conduct*), the accent is placed on the _____ syllable (first, second) when used as nouns and on the _____ syllable (first, second) when used as verbs.
first unaccented	**5.** In two-syllable words, the accent is usually placed on the _____ syllable (*clï mate*), unless the word begins (first, second) with a prefix (*a rise'*). Prefixes, such as the one in the word *arise*, are _____ . (accented, unaccented)
<u>an</u>nounce, <u>con</u>spire, <u>un</u>real, <u>ig</u>nore, <u>pro</u>claim unaccented accented ignore, proclaim	**6.** All of the following words contain prefixes. Read them aloud and underline the prefixes that are unaccented. *an nounce con spire un real ig nore pro claim* In words containing prefixes, the prefix is generally _____ , and the root word is generally (accented, unaccented) _____. (accented, unaccented) The vowel graphemes in prefixes do not always represent the schwa phoneme. Which of the words above do not contain the schwa sound? _____

*farm′er, short′est,
laugh′ing, joy′ful,
glad′ness, fool′ish,
point′less, wait′er*
unaccented

accented

7. All of the following words contain suffixes or inflectional endings. Read them aloud and write the accent mark over the accented syllable in each word.

farm er   short est   laugh ing   joy ful   glad ness
fool ish   point less   wait er

In words containing suffixes, the suffix is generally
_____ , and the root word is generally
(accented, unaccented)
_____ .
(accented, unaccented)

---

robbed   bagged

wished   kissed

seated   loaded

root word

8. The inflectional ending *ed* is not always a syllable. Read the following words aloud: *wished, kissed, robbed, bagged, seated, loaded.* The ending *ed* represents the phoneme /d/ in the words _____ and _____ because it follows voiced consonants. The *ed* ending represents the phoneme /t/ in the words _____ and _____ because it follows voiceless consonants. The *ed* ending represents the syllable /ud/ in the words _____ and _____ because it follows either a *t* or a *d.* When the *ed* ending represents a syllable, the accent is placed on the _____ .
(ending, root word)

---

na
des

9. Words consisting of three or more syllables are likely to have both a primary accent and a secondary accent. In the word *des ti na tion,* the primary accent is on the syllable _____ , and the secondary accent is on the syllable _____ .

me, o, m pre sion schwa	**10.** In words of more than two syllables, accented and unaccented syllables usually alternate with each other. In the word *me tab o lis m*, the three unaccented syllables are _____, _____, and _____ . In the word *com pre hen sion*, the two unaccented syllables are _____ and _____ . The vowels in all of the unaccented syllables in these words represent the _____ phoneme.
grav i ta′ tion, ex ten′ sion, sym pa thet′ ic, ex pen′ sive, fric′tion, con vul′ sion	**11.** In most multisyllabic words ending in *tion, sion, ic,* and *sive,* the primary accent falls on the syllable preceding these endings. Place the primary accent on the following words (notice the stress and schwa pattern of alternation): grav i ta tion ex ten sion sym pa thet ic ex pen sive fric tion con vul sion
vol′un tar y, col′um nist, har′mo nize, op′ti mis m, cru′ci fy, grat′i tude, ge og′ra phy, cel′ e brate, lav′a tor y	**12.** In most multisyllabic words ending in *ary, ist, ize, ism, fy, tude, y, ate,* and *tory,* the primary accent falls on the syllable before the syllable preceding these endings. Place the primary accent on the following words: vol un tar y col um nist har mo nize op ti mis m cru ci fy grat i tude ge og ra phy cel e brate lav a tor y
im pec′ ca ble, e mer′ gen cy, an′ i mal, A mer′ i can, var′ i ous, dif′ fer ent, sim′ i lar, av′ er age, ad′ jec tive, dis′ tance, sen′ tence, pos′ si ble	**13.** In most multisyllabic words ending in *al, an, ent/ant, ous, ar, ence/ance, able/ible, age, tive,* and *ency/ancy,* the primary accent falls on the syllable before the syllable preceding the ending if there is only one consonant before the suffix. If there are two consonants before the suffix, the primary accent falls on the syllable preceding the ending. Place the primary accent on the following words: im pec ca ble e mer gen cy an i mal A mer i can var i ous dif fer ent sim i lar av er age ad jec tive dis tance sen tence pos si ble

(A)(B)(C) **Review 15**   **1.** What is a syllable?

2. The number of vowel sounds you hear in a word equals _____.

3. We can "feel" syllables because _____.

4. Why study syllabication?

5. Explain the concept of accented and unaccented syllables.

6. When *y* occurs in the accented syllable, it represents the _____ phoneme, and when it occurs in the unaccented syllable it represents the _____ phoneme.

7. Where is the accent generally placed in compound words?

8. Where is the accent generally placed in words containing prefixes, suffixes, and inflectional endings?

9. Where is the accent generally placed in two-syllable words?

10. When is the *ed* inflectional ending a syllable?

11. State the accent generalization for words ending in the suffixes *tion, sion, ic,* and *sive.*

12. State the accent generalization for words ending in the suffixes *ary, ist, ize, ism, fy, tude, y, ate,* and *tory.*

13. State the accent generalization for words ending in the suffixes *al, an, ent/ant, ous, ar, ence/ance, able/ible, age, tive,* and *ency/ancy.*

See the Answers section for the answers to Review 15.

Syllable Division Clues

patterns	**1.** The most important issue in syllabication for the reading teacher is where the syllabic divisions occur. This information is important to beginning readers because phonics knowledge loses its effectiveness when applied to words of more than one syllable if the syllable _____ in multisyllabic words (accents, patterns) are not perceived.

vowel
 	
one
 	
VCe
 	
vowel team
	2. The approach to the division of syllables taken in this text is different from traditional approaches. The approach is simple, but linguistically sound. The key to syllabication is the _____ . Each syllable contains
	        (vowel, beginning consonants)
	_____ vowel phoneme, even though it may contain more
	(How many?)
	than one vowel letter. The two syllable patterns containing more than one vowel letter are the _____ pattern and
	                              (closed, VCe)
	the _____ pattern.
	     (open, vowel team)

represent phonemes one silent silent phoneme	**3.** Since each syllable contains only one vowel sound, we can first identify the number of syllables in a word if we can identify the number of vowels in the word that _____ . In order to do this we must (represent phonemes, are silent) know that vowel teams represent _____ phoneme/s, (How many?) the *e* vowel in VCe syllables is _____ , the *e* in *dge* and *ge* graphemes at the end of words is _____ , the letter *y* represents a vowel _____ when it isn't used to begin words or syllables, and the letters *le* at the end of multisyllabic words represent the syllable /ul/.
consonant /j/	**4.** We must also know that when the letters *ci* and *ti* are followed by vowels (*facial*, *direction*), they represent _____ phonemes, and that when the letters *gi* and (vowel, consonant) *ge* are followed by vowels (*legion*, *pigeon*), those letters represent the phoneme _____ . When we know *when* vowel graphemes represent vowel phonemes, we can identify the number of syllables in a word by just looking at it.

distance, finally, thousand, explain, firsthand, discharge, complete syllables	**5.** Underline all of the vowels or vowel teams that represent one phoneme in the following words: *distance finally thousand explain* *firsthand discharge complete* The number of vowels or vowel teams that you have underlined in each word equals the number of _____ in that word.
phonemes	**6.** A beginning point for the identification of syllable boundaries, then, is to locate the vowels that represent _____ .

two
 	
two
	7. Once you are able to identify the vowel letters representing phonemes in words, you are ready to discover some basic linguistic patterns related to syllabication. Study the words in each column below:
	
	Column 1 **Column 2**
	admit *fever*
	butter *label*
	complete *pilot*
	athlete *ether*
	unchain *wagon*
	discharge *seven*
	harmful *level*
	                 whether
	
	All of the words in both columns contain _____
	                                   (How many?)
	vowel phonemes. All of the words have _____
	                                   (How many?)
	syllables.

two or more one	**8.** Look again at the words in frame 7. The words in Column 1 have _____ consonant letter(s) between the vowels (How many?) representing vowel phonemes. The words in Column 2 have _____ consonant letter(s) between the vowels (How many?) representing vowel phonemes. *Key:* Multisyllabic words have either one consonant unit between vowels representing phonemes or they have two or more. (Consonant units are consonants or consonant digraphs.)
but ter, com plete, *ath lete, un chain* *dis charge, harm ful*	**9.** Continue to study the words in frame 7. Focus on the words in Column 1. Notice that when two or more consonant units separate vowels representing phonemes (*admit*), the first syllable ends after the first consonant unit (*ad*), and the second syllable begins with whatever consonant units are left (*mit*). Write the syllable divisions for the rest of the words in Column 1 of frame 7:_____ _____ _____
consonant	**10.** Our first syllabication generalization is: When there are two or more consonant units between vowels representing phonemes, the first syllable ends after the first _____ unit.

one	**11.** Look at the words in Column 2 in frame 7. All of these words have _____ consonant unit(s) between vowels 　　　　　(How many?) representing phonemes. However, the first syllable ends after the first vowel in the first four words (*fe ver, la bel, pi lot, e ther*), while the first syllable ends after the consonant unit in the last four words (*wheth er, wag on, sev en, lev el*). When the first
open	syllable ends after the vowel, that syllable is _____ , 　　　　　　　　　　　　　　　　　　(open, closed) and the vowel in the syllable represents its long sound. When the first syllable ends after the consonant unit, that syllable is
short	closed, and the vowel in the syllable represents its _____ sound.
consonant unit	**12.** Fifty-five percent of the time that one consonant unit separates vowels representing phonemes, the first syllable ends after the vowel, and 45 percent of the time, the first syllable ends after the _____ .
shi ny, mer chant, pu pil, spi der, frol ic, gav el, bish op, chap el	**13.** Our second syllabication generalization is: When there is one consonant unit between vowels representing phonemes, divide the syllable after the first vowel and pronounce the word. If it doesn't make sense, divide the syllable after the consonant unit. Write the syllable divisions for the following words using this generalization: *shiny, merchant, pupil, spider, frolic, gavel, bishop, chapel* _____ _____ _____

/ul/ one there are two consonant units between the *le* and the vowel preceding it.	**14.** A special linguistic pattern involves the use of *le* at the end of multisyllabic words (*maple, babble, candle, able, bugle*). In these situations, the *le* represents a syllable, and the *le* syllable represents the phonemes _____ . Once you realize that the *le* grapheme represents a syllable, you simply look at the *le*, the vowel before it, and the number of consonant units between the two, and you can apply either of our generalizations to find the syllable division. For example, in the word *maple* there is/are _____ consonant unit/s <div align="center">(one, two)</div>between the *le* and the vowel *a*, so I can use the second generalization to find the syllable boundaries. I would use the first generalization to find the syllable boundaries in the word *babble* because _____ _____
tick le, no ble, fid dle, *ca ble, tat tle*	**15.** Use the appropriate generalization to help you find the syllable divisions for the following words: *tickle, noble, fiddle, cable, tattle.* _____ _____
syllables	**16.** Combine your knowledge of prefixes and suffixes with your knowledge of the two syllabication generalizations, and the ease with which you find the syllable divisions in multisyllabic words increases. Prefixes (**a**lone) and suffixes (*venge**ful***) are often separate _____ , but not always (*agree**able***).

ary, ism, tory, able/ible, ency/ancy	**17.** Examine the following suffixes that are most often used in words of more than two syllables and write those that are not separate syllables: *ion, sion, ic, sive, ary, ist, ize, ism, fy, tude, y, ate, tory, al, an, ent/ant, ous, ar, ence/ance, able/ible, age, tive,* and *ency/ancy.*_____ _____ _____
ble *schwa*	*impossible terrible responsible vegetable available* **18.** The suffixes *able* and *ible* are divided between the vowel and the letters _____ , and the vowels *a* and *i* usually represent the _____ phoneme.
/âr/ */ē/*	*necessary dictionary ordinary library military* **19.** The suffix *ary* is divided between the *ar* and the *y* and the *ar* grapheme represents the phoneme _____ , while the *y* grapheme represents the phoneme _____ .
or *y* */ur/*	*history factory victory laboratory territory dormitory* **20.** The suffix *ory* is divided between the _____ and the _____ , and the *or* grapheme represents /ur/ or /or/ depending on the accent. When the *or* and *ar* graphemes are in the unaccented syllable (*col**or**, buzz**ard***), they represent the phoneme _____ .
n c *s m*	*frequency occupancy optimism hypnotism* **21.** The suffixes *ency/ancy* are divided between the letters _____ and _____ , while the suffix *ism* is divided between the letters _____ and _____ . A schwa phoneme is inserted between the graphemes *is* (/iz/) and *m* (/um/).

	painted wanted landed handed **22.** Remember that the *ed* inflectional ending is only a syllable when it is preceded by the letters _____ or _____ .
t d	
	famous tremendous information direction television division **23.** The suffixes *ous, tion,* and *sion* are used so frequently in multisyllabic words that it is helpful to look for these syllable units and to learn the phonemes that each represents. The *ous* grapheme represents the phonemes _____ , the *tion* grapheme usually represents the phonemes _____ , and the *sion* grapheme represents the phonemes _____ .
/us/ /shun/ /shun/	
	24. Finally, if you want to become very skilled in syllable division, add to everything you have learned, the accent and schwa pattern of alternation discussed under Accent Placement Clues earlier in the Accent Placement Clues section of this text.

Answer the questions in Review 16. Then you will be ready for the posttest. Good luck!

 Review 16 **1.** Where do we begin the task of identifying syllable boundaries?

2. What must we know in order to determine visually which vowel letters in words represent vowel sounds?

3. After we have identified the vowel graphemes representing phonemes in a word, how do we determine the syllable boundaries?

See the Answers section for answers to Review 16.

Self-Evaluation: A Posttest ___

This test will help you evaluate your growth in phonics knowledge and issues related to phonics. Read each item carefully, including all of the choices. Circle the letter (a, b, c, d, or e) to indicate your best answer. Be sure to respond to all test items.

I. Multiple Choice. Select the best answer.

1. Which of the following most adequately completes the sentence? Language can be
 a. either associative or communicative.
 b. either expressive or receptive.
 c. either oral or written.
 d. All of the above.
 e. Both b and c.

2. Which of the following most adequately completes the sentence? The major reason we study phonics is to
 a. learn about consonant and vowel sounds.
 b. learn how to sound out words.
 c. learn how the spoken language relates to the written language.
 d. become phonemically aware.
 e. Both b and c.

3. How many phonemes are in the word *lunch?*
 a. one   **b.** two   **c.** four   **d.** six   **e.** seven

4. How many graphemes are in the word *lunch?*
 a. one   **b.** two   **c.** four   **d.** six   **e.** seven

5. Which of the following most adequately completes the sentence? The meanings young readers acquire from reading are largely based on
 a. written context.
 b. prosody.
 c. decoding.
 d. their knowledge of spoken words.
 e. phonics.

6. Which of the following most adequately completes the sentence? The written language is
 a. difficult to understand.
 b. as easy to acquire as the oral language.
 c. used more often in schools than the oral language.
 d. a representation of the oral language.
 e. a primary language form.

7. Which of the following statement(s) are correct?

   a. A phoneme is the written representation of a grapheme.
   b. A grapheme is the written representation of a phoneme.
   c. A phoneme is the smallest unit of sound in a word.
   d. *Grapheme* and *letter* are synonymous terms.
   e. Statements b and c are correct.

8. Which of the following statement(s) are correct?

   a. The letter *x* has no sound of its own.
   b. The letter *c* has no sound of its own.
   c. The letters *y* and *w* are used to represent both consonant and vowel phonemes.
   d. The letter *q* has no sound of its own.
   e. All of the statements above are correct.

9. Which of the following most adequately completes the sentence? The differences in the meaning that we associate with spoken words are affected mostly by

   a. graphemes.
   b. phonemes.
   c. syllables.
   d. phonological awareness.
   e. syntax.

10. Which of the following most adequately completes the sentence? If we didn't have a written language, there would be little reason to

   a. learn about syntax.
   b. study phonics.
   c. develop phonemic awareness.
   d. learn about text structure.
   e. Both b and c.

11. The letter *y* is most likely to be a consonant when

   a. it is the first letter in a word or syllable.
   b. it is the final letter in a word or syllable.
   c. it occurs in the middle of a syllable.
   d. it follows the letter *a* in a word or syllable.
   e. None of the above.

12. Which of the following most adequately completes the sentence? Most of the consonant speech sounds are predictably represented by

   a. 18 consonant letters and 5 consonant digraphs.
   b. 21 consonant letters.
   c. single-letter consonants and consonant blends.
   d. 21 consonant phonemes.
   e. The written form of the American English language is too irregular for any safe predictions.

13. The consonant digraph is illustrated by

    a. the *oa* in *soap*.
    b. the *th* in *with*.
    c. the *st* in *stop*.
    d. the *nt* in *bent*.
    e. the *gh* in *though*.

14. The voiced equivalent of the consonant sound represented by the *t* in *tie* is

    a. the consonant sound represented by the *d* in *dog*.
    b. the consonant sound represented by the *b* in *bug*.
    c. the consonant sound represented by the *g* in *go*.
    d. the consonant sound represented by the *v* in *van*.
    e. the consonant sound represented by the *z* in *zoo*.

15. The voiceless equivalent of the consonant sound represented by the *g* in *go* is

    a. the consonant sound represented by the *f* in *fun*.
    b. the consonant sound represented by the *s* in *sit*.
    c. the consonant sound represented by the *ch* in *chin*.
    d. the consonant sound represented by the *t* in *top*.
    e. the consonant sound represented by the *c* in *can*.

16. Which of the following most adequately completes the sentence? Consonant phonemes and graphemes are

    a. used in the middle of syllables.
    b. used at the beginning and ending of syllables.
    c. more important than vowel phonemes and graphemes.
    d. Both a and b.
    e. None of the above.

17. Which of the following most adequately completes the sentence? The consonant letter *q* is not really needed to represent consonant phonemes because

    a. it never occurs in words without the letter *u* after it.
    b. other letters represent the sound/s it represents.
    c. it looks too much like the letter *g*.
    d. Both a and b.
    e. All of the above.

18. The consonant letter *s* most frequently represents the sound/s heard in

    a. *ship*.   **b.** *zone*.   **c.** *sugar*.   **d.** *so*.   **e.** Both b and d

19. The word *laugh* ends with the same sound as the sound represented by

    a. the *f* in *of*.
    b. the *ph* in *graph*.
    c. the *gh* in *caught*.
    d. the *gh* in *ghost*.
    e. Both a and b.

20. The consonant letter _c_ followed by an _e_ is most likely to represent the same sound represented by

    a. the letter _c_ in _ocean._
    b. the letter _s_ in _some._
    c. the letter _c_ when followed by _o._
    d. the letter _c_ when followed by _i._
    e. Both b and d.

21. The consonant letter _g_ followed by a _u_ is most likely to represent the same sound represented by

    a. the _j_ in _jump._
    b. the _gh_ in _ghastly._
    c. the _g_ in _sing._
    d. the letter _g_ followed by _i._
    e. Both a and d.

22. The open syllable in the nonsense word _tamel_ would most likely rhyme with

    a. _ham._
    b. _pay._
    c. _fell._
    d. _game._
    e. _come._

23. A vowel diphthong is best illustrated by the vowels representing the sound of

    a. _oo_ in _took._
    b. _ou_ in _trout._
    c. _ai_ in _said._
    d. _oy_ in _joy._
    e. Both b and d.

24. The schwa sound is represented by

    a. the _ai_ in _certain._
    b. the _ay_ in _day._
    c. the _ou_ in _famous._
    d. the _e_ in _wished._
    e. Both a and c.

25. An example of a closed syllable is found in which of the following words?

    a. _mine_
    b. _me_
    c. _stretch_
    d. _high_
    e. _tea_

26. Which of the following has an incorrect diacritical mark?

    a. _tăll_   **b.** băck   **c.** _ŭp_   **d.** _dĭtch_   **e.** _pĭg_

27. Which of the following has an incorrect diacritical mark?

    a. *fūse*   **b.** *ĕve*   **c.** *tīme*   **d.** *lōve*   **e.** *stāge*

28. When the single vowel *a* is followed by a single consonant and a final *e*, the *a* would most likely have the sound of

    a. the *ai* in *aim*.
    b. the *a* in *have*.
    c. the *a* in *ball*.
    d. the *ay* in *day*.
    e. Both a and d.

29. If the vowel *o* was the only and final vowel in a syllable, the *o* would most likely represent the same sound as

    a. the *o* in *mother*.
    b. the *a* in *was*.
    c. the *o* in *do*.
    d. the *ew* in *sew*.
    e. None of the above.

30. If the single vowel *a* was in a syllable ending with one or more consonants, the *a* would most likely represent the same sound as

    a. the *ea* in *great*.
    b. the *ai* in *plaid*.
    c. the *a* in *fall*.
    d. the *au* in *gauge*.
    e. None of the above.

31. The word containing a murmur diphthong is

    a. *coat*.
    b. *bead*.
    c. *hurt*.
    d. *town*.
    e. *rail*.

32. When the letters *ai* appear together in a syllable, they usually represent the same sound as

    a. the *a* in *rag*.
    b. the *i* in *risk*.
    c. the *aw* in *lawn*.
    d. the *ey* in *they*.
    e. the *a* in *want*.

33. An example of a vowel team syllable is

    a. *game*.   **b.** *so*.   **c.** *stamp*.   **d.** *create*.   **e.** *coach*.

II. Multiple Choice. Select the word in each row in which the primary accent is correctly placed.

34. *permissible*   **a.** *per′missible*   **b.** *permis′sible*   **c.** *permissi′ble*   **d.** *permissible′*
35. *metropolitan*   **a.** *met′ropolitan*   **b.** *metro′politan*   **c.** *metropol′itan*   **d.** *metropoli′tan*
36. *appropriate*   **a.** *ap′propriate*   **b.** *appro′priate*   **c.** *appropri′ate*   **d.** *appropriate′*
37. *interruption*   **a.** *in′terruption*   **b.** *inter′ruption*   **c.** *interrup′tion*   **d.** *interruption′*

III. Multiple Choice. Select the word in each row that is incorrectly syllabicated.

38. **a.** *la bor*   **b.** *so da*   **c.** *gra vy*   **d.** *ca mel*   **e.** *de mon*
39. **a.** *em blem*   **b.** *com plete*   **c.** *bur den*   **d.** *ex cept*   **e.** *mons ter*
40. **a.** *merch an dise* **b.** *ath lete*   **c.** *e ther*   **d.** *watch ful*   **e.** *dis charge*
41. **a.** *re gion*   **b.** *pi rate*   **c.** *gi ant*   **d.** *page ant*   **e.** *treach er ous*
42. **a.** *sym pa thet ic* **b.** *con vul sion* **c.** *ge og ra phy* **d.** *im pec ca ble* **e.** *tre mend ous*

IV. Multiple Choice. Select the words in each item (a, b, c) that contain a sound that the letter or group of letters at the left might represent. If none of the words contain a sound represented by the letter or group of letters, mark e. If all of the words contain a sound represented by the letter or group of letters, mark d.

43. *ti*   **a.** *choose*   **b.** *wish*   **c.** *machine*   **d.** All   **e.** None
44. *ci*   **a.** *sharp*   **b.** *sip*   **c.** *session*   **d.** All   **e.** None
45. *ge*   **a.** *guess*   **b.** *jello*   **c.** *jump*   **d.** All   **e.** None
46. *ce*   **a.** *single*   **b.** *car*   **c.** *keep*   **d.** All   **e.** None

V. Multiple Choice. Select the word in each item (a, b, c) that contains the same sound as that represented by the underlined part of the word at the left. If none of the words contain that sound, mark e. If all of the words contain that sound, mark d.

47. <u>h</u>orse   **a.** *honor*   **b.** *whom*   **c.** *right*   **d.** All   **e.** None
48. m<u>oo</u>n   **a.** *few*   **b.** *cue*   **c.** *to*   **d.** All   **e.** None
49. <u>w</u>atch   **a.** *plow*   **b.** *who*   **c.** *once*   **d.** All   **e.** None
50. si<u>ng</u>   **a.** *ranger*   **b.** *tank*   **c.** *gem*   **d.** All   **e.** None

See page 207 for answers to Self-Evaluation: A Posttest.
Self-Evaluation: A Posttest   Number correct _____
Self-Evaluation: A Pretest   Number correct _____

Chapter 5

Teaching Phonics to Children

PHONICS KNOWLEDGE

The major purpose of this book is to enhance your knowledge of phonics; that is, to help you consciously understand the relationships between spoken and written language. If you have carefully studied the material presented so far, you have learned how American English speech sounds are represented by an alphabetic code in written words. This knowledge should help you become a better teacher.

Knowledgeable teachers, in any area of study, tend to make wiser instructional decisions than less knowledgeable teachers, simply because they have a better understanding of what they are teaching. You have probably sensed by now that not all phonics knowledge is of equal importance. If you have, you will probably make good decisions about what phonics patterns and principles should be taught to children. If you haven't, then you will want to read this, and the remaining part of the book, very carefully. There are some phonics principles and patterns outlined for you in the first section of the text that you will not want to teach to all children. There are even some that you may not want to teach to any child. You might ask then, "Why go into so much detail?" My answers to that question are, "The more you know about phonics, the clearer your perceptions will be about what is and what is not critical to teach children," and "Since you must be able to respond intelligently to the many questions children ask as they learn about phonics, it is important for you to understand more about phonics than you intend to teach."

The decisions classroom teachers make about phonics instruction have far-reaching effects on children's literacy development. Some teachers spend so much time teaching children phonics that they have little time left for reading and writing. Children in these classrooms are often deprived of opportunities to enjoy good literature and to "use" the written language as it was meant to be used. Their literacy development is often slow, and their motivation for learning how to read and write is often poor. Other teachers totally ignore the teaching of phonics, or give it little conscious attention in their instructional programs. Children in these classrooms are often left to discover the alphabetic principle on their own—an extremely difficult task for many children. Because children in these classrooms are deprived of meaningful opportunities to develop phonemic awareness and phonics knowledge, the literacy development of some of them is often hindered, their self-images are generally low, and their attitudes toward reading and writing are often poor.

Effective literacy teachers never teach children everything they know about phonics. They teach them only what they need to know in order to develop a good understanding of the alphabetic principle—the basic principle on which reading and writing is based. However, they also recognize that phonics knowledge facilitates word recognition growth, word recognition growth affects reading fluency, and reading fluency affects reading comprehension. Therefore, effective literacy teachers do not avoid the teaching of phonics either!

Finally, effective teachers strive for a balanced literacy program. They seek for balance in learning to read and write, learning to enjoy reading and writing, and learning to use reading and writing in functional ways. In the "learning to read and write" area, they also seek for a balance of focus on "lower-order" and "higher-order" processes; that is, they try to balance their instruction so that children learn both the lower-order processes of decoding and encoding written language, and the higher-order processes of constructing and reconstructing written discourse. They recognize that the mastery of encoding and decoding makes it possible for individuals to engage independently in the higher-level processes. Therefore, they give proper attention to children's development in this area. They also recognize, however, that the enhancement of basic-, connecting-, and controlling-thinking processes and language/schemata does not have to be delayed until the lower-order processes are mastered. Therefore, they begin the development of these higher-order processes (assisting children to read material that they can't read by themselves), while at the same time introducing the lower-order processes.

In short, effective literacy teachers know that skilled readers (1) are automatic decoders; (2) employ both bottom-up and top-down strategies to make sense of print; (3) understand language (schemata/vocabulary, figurative language, parsing, prosodic features of print); (4) read between and beyond lines of print; (5) have multiple reading rates; (6) are able to focus on the "big" ideas presented in written text and perceive how those ideas relate to each other; and (7) control their own comprehension of written text. Since effective teachers have a clear vision of the end product of literacy instruction, they provide a balanced literacy program that focuses on all seven areas of development. While phonics knowledge is important in this whole process, it should never overshadow other important areas of knowledge.

PHONICS INSTRUCTION

A secondary purpose of this book is to introduce you to various phonics activities designed to help children develop their own strategies for identifying written words while also enhancing their word recognition abilities. These activities are presented in the next section of the book.

The teaching of phonics has been, and will probably always be, a topic surrounded with controversy. Suggestions for teaching phonics are many and varied. Some are effective in terms of their impact on children's reading growth, and some are not. Some are efficient in terms of the classroom time taken for this purpose, and some are not. The teaching of phonics is a subject I have treated extensively elsewhere (see Eldredge, J. L. *Teaching Decoding in Holistic Classrooms.* [1995]. Upper Saddle River, New Jersey: Merrill/Prentice Hall), and a full treatment of the topic is beyond the scope of this book. However, some simple, basic teaching activities that are very effective in helping children learn how to use phonics in reading and writing are not beyond the scope of this book. These activities are outlined for you in the next section. They are easy to teach, children enjoy them, and they work!

If you want to pursue other dimensions of phonics instruction, I would invite you to read *Teaching Decoding in Holistic Classrooms.* In this book, strategies for teaching phonics in the context of children's reading materials are described. This is a common, effective practice, if done correctly. Furthermore, suggestions for teaching phonics "out of context" are also presented in the book.

Although sentiment, at times, is against teaching phonics "out of context," there are some legitimate reasons for ignoring that sentiment. First, research supports the effectiveness of the practice. Second, research reveals that children do not find it meaningless, as some individuals claim. Third, research reveals that children enjoy it instead of dislike it, as some suggest. In sum, research findings reveal that brief "out of context" phonics instruction in an otherwise predominantly holistic environment improves children's reading achievement, helps them understand how print and speech are related, and is associated with positive attitudes toward reading. A discussion of this research is presented in *Teaching Decoding in Holistic Classrooms.*

The decision to teach phonics in or out of context is a choice that you must make for yourself. You may elect to do some of both. When using either approach, explain to children that learning about phonics helps them become better readers, but phonics by itself is not reading. Reading involves much more than just learning phonics.

Explicit phonics instruction need not take much classroom time. Daily ten-minute periods of systematic phonics instruction are adequate, if teachers focus on the right things.

Effective phonics instruction (1) need not absorb much classroom time; (2) will not communicate to children that phonics is reading; (3) can avoid phoneme distortion; (4) will be offered as a strategy to be used, not just skills to be learned; (5) can help children determine vowel sounds in words by syllable patterns; (6) will help children sound out words; (7) can be accomplished without the use of workbooks or ditto masters; (8) should be based on sound linguistic principles; and (9) will support holistic classrooms.

Phonics should be taught as a strategy for children to use rather than just skills for them to learn. Children can use phonics knowledge along with syntax and vocabulary knowledge to strategically decode unfamiliar words through contextual analysis. This decoding strategy is important for children to develop. However, phonics knowledge can also be used by children to strategically sound out words. I teach children to use the following strategy when identifying a word by sounds: First, determine the vowel sound in the unknown word (the syllable pattern or the vowel team pattern helps here). Second, blend the consonant sound before the vowel sound with the vowel sound (this eliminates any phoneme distortion). Third, isolate the consonant sound after the vowel sound. Fourth, blend everything together. For example, if using the strategy with the word *jump,* you would first determine the vowel sound. The word is a closed syllable word, so the vowel sound is short. The vowel sound is /u/. Second, blend the consonant sound before the vowel sound with the vowel sound: /ju/. Third, isolate the consonant sound after the vowel sound: /m-p/. Fourth, blend everything together: /ju/ /m-p/ = /jump/.

I teach children to use this phonics strategy only when it is appropriate. If they are able to recognize a word by sight, there is no reason to sound it out. Furthermore, words should not be sounded out if children are able to identify them by analogy, or by the contextual information provided in the sentence, since these identification strategies are much more efficient to use than phonics. However, if children do not recognize a written word, and if they cannot identify it by analogy or context, then the strategy should be used.

When teaching phonics to very young children who have not yet developed the ability to hear all of the phonemes in spoken words, I use rhyming books and games to help children develop "rhyming awareness" and "onset awareness." Children learn to associate the single consonant letters in rhyming words with the consonant sounds representing them at the same time they are developing the "phonemic awareness" abilities needed for successful reading and writing. It is only after children experience success with onsets and rimes that I introduce the phonics strategy to them.

I use the principles of social mediation, zone of proximal development, and scaffolding as I teach children to use the phonics strategy. That is, I do with them what they are incapable of doing for themselves until they are able to perform without my help. (See *Teaching Decoding in Holistic Classrooms* for a complete discussion of these principles.)

While I am teaching children how to develop the strategy for sounding out words, I introduce them to the phonics elements and patterns in the following simple sequence:

1. Five short vowel sounds
2. Initial consonant sounds (the most predictable sound associated with each consonant)
3. Vowel principles (determining long and short vowel sounds by syllable pattern)
4. Vowel teams (determining vowel sounds by letter clusters—most predictable sounds)
5. Final consonant sounds (The most predictable sound associated with each consonant)
6. Consonant digraph sounds (The most predictable sounds associated with each digraph)
7. Consonant blends
8. The letter *y* as a vowel

The ten-minute phonics instruction, outlined in *Teaching Decoding in Holistic Classrooms* and briefly described above, is succinct, systematic, and intensive. It complements holistic, informal decoding strategies such as the shared book experience, shared music experience, shared rhythm experience, group assisted reading, dyad reading, tape assisted reading, and the Language Experience Approach (LEA). It also complements holistic writing experiences in which children use invented spelling while they are moving toward the orthographic stage of reading acquisition.

Part Two

Classroom Phonics Activities

Chapter 6

Developmental Stages
of Decoding

There are many ways to decode written words (translate written words into language). Proficient readers have learned to perform this task by a process called "word recognition"; they recognize written words by their spellings. When good readers do not recognize written words, they generally identify them by analogy or by context. However, beginning or poor readers cannot use these word identification strategies because their "sight" word vocabularies are too small.

Unless a sufficient number of written words are stored in the memory of a reader, the identification of unfamiliar words by analogy or context is impossible. When readers identify words by analogy, they search in their lexical memory for a word that contains the same rime (c**an,** m**an,** t**an,** r**an,** etc.) or beginning (**ba**ck, **ba**t, **ba**nd, **ba**d, etc.) so unfamiliar words (**ban,** for example) can be identified. If the number of sight words in memory is insufficient, the identification of unfamiliar words by analogy is difficult, if not impossible.

When readers identify words by contextual analysis, they use various language cues to make logical guesses. They use syntax cues, which suggest the function of the unfamiliar word (Is it naming something? Is it describing something? Is it describing some action?); graphophonic cues, (which indicate the beginning sound of the unfamiliar word); and semantic cues, which indicate whether certain words would make sense in a particular sentence. For example, in the sentence "The dog b_____ at the cat," the reader might identify the unknown word *barked* by thinking "What action word beginning with the letter *b* would make sense in this sentence?" If the reader could not read all of the words around the word *barked*, then the use of context for the identification of that word would be impossible.

When we teach phonics to emerging readers, we equip them with a necessary tool for identifying words by context. More important, however, we also equip them with the tools needed to identify unfamiliar words by their letter-sound sequences (i.e., we teach them how to "sound out" unfamiliar words). This is an important, practical skill for young readers to acquire. However, it is not the primary reason for teaching phonics to young children.

Phonics knowledge equips children with the tools they need to remember a word's spelling sequence. A word's spelling sequence sets it apart from all other words, and it is this sequence that we store in lexical memory so we can recognize it. Therefore, the primary purpose for teaching phonics to children is to help them develop their word recognition abilities.

Recent research indicates that children go through predictable developmental stages in sounding out written words. These stages are closely related to their developmental spelling stages, and directly related to their levels of phonemic awareness. The findings of this research help teachers understand how children learn to sound out unfamiliar words, and they also provide teachers with important information regarding appropriate phonics activities for children at various stages of development.

Since children have not developed strategies for sounding out words when they first begin to read, they try to remember written words by some visual feature/s. When they begin to develop sounding-out strategies, however, the first words they are able to decode are simple, single-syllable words—words beginning with a single consonant, containing only one vowel, and ending with a single consonant (examples, *man, big, sit*, etc.). Research findings indicate they learn to decode these consonant-vowel-consonant (CVC) words before they are able to sound out words containing consonant digraphs (*sh, th*, etc.), consonant blends (*bl, st*, etc.), vowel teams (*oa* as in *soap, ai* as in *rain*, etc.), and words organized in a CVe pattern (*bone, came*, etc.).

The first CVC words children are able to decode contain predictable consonant letters in the initial and final positions. They are unable to sound out words beginning with a *q* or with a *c* that represents /s/ until much later. You have already learned that the letter *q* is paired with a *u* in words (*quit, quiet*), and the letter *c* represents /s/ when it is followed by an *e, i,* or *y* (*cent, rice, city, cycle*), so when these letters occur in words, they are not really simple CVC words. The easiest consonants for children to decode in CVC words are *n, b, t, z, l, p, m, f, k, x* representing /ks/, *c* representing /k/, *d, r, s, h, j, g* representing either /g/ or /j/, *y*, and *w*. The most difficult consonants for children to decode in CVC words are *v, qu,* and *c* representing /s/.

The ability to sound out words containing consonant digraphs (*ch, sh,* etc.) and blends (*st, fl,* etc.) occurs **after** children develop the ability to decode CVC words. Words containing the *sh* digraph seem to be the easiest for young children to decode, followed by words containing *ch* and *ng*. The easiest consonant blends for children to decode in the initial position of words seem to be *sl* and *fl*, and the easiest consonant blends for children to decode in the final position of words seem to be *ft* and *st*.

Children develop the ability to sound out words containing simple vowel teams (*keep*) before they are able to consistently decode words in the VCe pattern (*hope*). However, children have more difficulty with some vowel teams than others, so there isn't a clear trend suggesting that vowel team words are easier for children to decode than VCe words. Children find it difficult to decode words containing *y* as a vowel, but the most difficult words for children to decode are those containing complex consonant clusters (*ranch, scratch, graph, stretch,* etc.) and silent letters (*know, write, gnat*).

The most important findings of the developmental decoding stages data are

1. Children go through predictable developmental decoding stages, and children's decoding growth follows a consistent pattern from grade one through grade three.

2. Children's ability to sound out words closely parallels their developmental spelling stages, and is dependent on their levels of phonemic awareness.

3. Children are able to sound out simple CVC words before they are able to sound out words containing consonant clusters (blends and digraphs), and before they are able to decode VCe words and words containing vowel teams.

4. The most difficult words for children to sound out are those containing difficult vowel teams (*oi, ou*), complex consonant clusters (*squ, scr, str, nge, ph*), and silent letters (*gn, wr, kn*).

5. Children's ability to sound out words is significantly related to their overall word recognition abilities, their reading fluency, and their reading comprehension.

We now realize that phonics knowledge is needed for optimal sight word recognition growth. Sight word learning is not a paired-associate memory process, as originally believed, but a process involving the establishment of systematic connections between the spellings and pronunciations of words. Phonics knowledge facilitates these connections.

Reading is a complex process involving the use of many knowledge sources. Phonics knowledge is just one of those sources. Phonics knowledge, however, contributes significantly to a person's overall decoding ability, and without the ability to translate the written text into language, readers could not access their vocabulary, syntax, schemata, or discourse knowledge to construct meaning.

The teaching activities that follow are based on "phonemic awareness" research (research suggesting how children develop the ability to hear phonemes in spoken words), phonics knowledge research, and research on children's developmental stages of decoding.

Chapter 7

Early Experiences with Written Text

READING BOOKS WITH CHILDREN

It is a well-established fact that reading books to and with children positively impacts their reading growth. The early, enjoyable experiences children have with books provide them with the motivation to learn to read. If children are able to see the text while it is being read, and if parents and teachers track the print with a finger as they read the story with emotion and expression, the reading experience is even more valuable. From these early reading experiences with written text young children learn the important concepts they need to read independently. Some of these important concepts are that (1) written words represent spoken words; (2) alphabetic letters are used to make written words; (3) written words are read from the left to the right, and from the top to the bottom; (4) the spaces that separate written words are larger than the spaces that separate letters within written words; and (5) punctuation marks help us know when to raise the pitch of our voice, stress words, and pause while reading.

One of the most important concepts for young children to learn is word awareness. Word awareness refers to our ability to perceive individual words. The syllable is the smallest pronunciation unit in the language; that is, syllables are the sound units we hear as we speak. Some words are made of only one syllable, but other words are comprised of two, three, or more syllables. These multisyllabic words confuse us as we seek to understand a spoken language. As we listen to the pronunciation units (syllables) in speech, we might say to ourselves, "Does the sound I just heard end the word, or is it the beginning of another word?" Young children reveal this confusion when they ask teachers to help them spell such words as *gimme* (rather than *give me*), or *wanta* (rather than *want a*).

Children must be able to develop word awareness with the spoken language before, or at the same time as, they develop word awareness with the written language. In the written language, the spaces between written words separates them. Children must be able to match spoken words with the written ones representing them in order to read. One of the most effective ways to help children develop word awareness is to read them stories. I will demonstrate a word awareness activity shortly.

Another important concept related to the ability to read independently and the development of phonics knowledge is rhyme awareness. Children develop an awareness of rhyming words before they develop an awareness of a word's beginning phonemes. In fact, after children have developed rhyme awareness it is easy to introduce them to their first phonics activities. You can use rhyming words beginning with various consonant sounds to teach children the relationships between the first letter of a word and the phoneme it represents.

To illustrate a variety of activities you can use with a story to develop children's awareness of both words and rhymes, I have written an alphabet book (Figure 1) that can be made into a "big" book. Books with large print are useful for teaching beginning reading concepts because all of the children in the classroom can see the words and punctuation marks in the book as it is read with them. As the print is tracked by the teacher, children can also develop the concepts of left-to-right and top-to-bottom directionality.

Not only is an alphabet book useful for teaching word and rhyme awareness, but it can also be used to help children learn the names of the alphabet letters and the sounds that are represented by them.

USING BOOKS TO DEVELOP WORD AWARENESS

On large cards, draw pictures of the key words used in *Alphabet Sounds.* (If you prefer, you can cut out the pictures from magazines or old workbooks.) Underneath each picture, write the key word. The noun pictures you should have are: *bug, cat, cake, duck, meat, fish, girl, squirrel, hair, kid* (baby goat), *lamp, coat, milk, nut, hat, ox, pup, ring, rake, bat, chair, top, bear, van, zoo,* and *tree.* You will need to be a little creative to draw pictures of someone sitting in a chair (*sit*); someone jumping (*jump*); someone running (*run*); someone baking (*bake*); someone waking up (*wake*); the edge of a trampoline, mountain, or bed (*edge*); and a curl of smoke, wood, or hair (*curl*). Some words are difficult to illustrate, so pictures will not be used. However, a card should be made for each of those words: *at, itch, quit, us, other, brother,* "ks," *you,* and *me.* (Although some of the words are hard to illustrate, the words chosen for the alphabet rhyming book, particularly the vowel words, were carefully selected for purposes that will be explained later.)

Show each picture card to the children and tell them the word that goes with each one. Distribute the picture cards to various children and ask them to hold up the appropriate card when the right word is read. As you read *Alphabet Sounds* with the children, teach them to add voice and facial expressions, plus hand and arm movements, to make the experience enjoyable and meaningful.

Before you begin to read the first two lines of *Alphabet Sounds,* ask the children with the *at, bug,* and *cat* cards to come to the front of the class and stand next to the big book. Line them up in the order their words will

---

Alphabet Sounds
by J. Lloyd Eldredge

A is for **at,** imagine that!
B is for **bug,** but not for cat.

C is for **cake,** something good to eat.
D is for **duck,** but not for meat.

E is for **edge,** but don't fall off!
F is for **fish,** but not for cough.

G is for **girl,** and not for squirrel.
H is for **hair,** but not for curl.

I is for **itch,** that's not fun!
J is for **jump,** but not for run.

K is for **kid,** a baby goat.
L is for **lamp,** but not for coat.

M is for **milk,** cows make that!
N is for **nut,** but not for hat.

P is for **pup,** but not for ring.
O is for **ox,** who pulls anything.

Q is for **quit,** I won't do that!
R is for **rake,** but not for bat.

S is for **sit,** I love my chair!
T is for **top,** but not for bear.

U is for **us,** we love each other!
V is for **van,** but not for brother.

W is for **wake,** and not for bake.
X is for "**ks,**" a sound fun to make.

Y is for **you,** and not for me.
Z is for **zoo,** but not for tree.

Figure 1

appear. As you read the first part of line 1 (**A** is for **at**), the child who has the *at* word card should hold it up when the word is said. When the second part of line 1 is read (imagine that!), all of the children should throw their hands up in the air. As you read the second line (**B** is for **bug,** but not for cat), the children who have the *bug* and *cat* word cards should hold them up when they are said.

Before reading the next two lines of *Alphabet Sounds,* ask the children with the *cake, duck,* and *meat* cards to come to the front of the class and stand next to the big book. Line them up in the order their words will appear. While you read the first part of line 3 (**C** is for **cake**), the child who has the *cake* word card should hold it up when the word is said. When the second part of line 3 is read (something good to eat), all of the children should rub their stomachs and smack their lips together. As you read the fourth line (**D** is for **duck,** but not for meat), the children who have the *duck* and *meat* word cards should hold them up when they are said.

The children with the *edge* and *fish* cards should come to the front of the class and stand next to the big book, in the order their words will appear, before the next two lines are read. As you read the first part of line 5 (**E** is for **edge**), the child who has the *edge* word card should hold it up when the word is said. When the second part of line 5 is read (but don't fall off!), all of the children should pretend they are jumping away from some edge. As you read the first part of line 6 (**F** is for **fish**), the child who has the *fish* word card should hold it up when it is said. When the second part of line 6 is read (but not for cough), all of the children should cough.

Ask the children with the *girl, squirrel, hair,* and *curl* cards to come to the front of the class and stand next to the big book, in the order their words will appear, before you begin to read the next two lines of *Alphabet Sounds.* As you read these lines (**G** is for **girl,** and not for squirrel. **H** is for **hair,** but not for curl), the children who have the word cards should hold them up as they are read.

The children with the *itch, jump,* and *run* cards should come to the front of the class and stand next to the big book, in the order their words will appear, for the next two lines. As you read the first part of line 9 (**I** is for **itch**), the child who has the *itch* word card should hold it up when the word is said. When the second part of line 9 is read (that's not fun!), all of the children should scratch themselves on the shoulder and repeatedly turn their heads to the left and right. As you read the first part of line 10 (**J** is for **jump**), the child who has the *jump* card should hold it up, and all of the children should jump in the air, once. As the second part of line 10 is read (but not for run), the child who has the *run* word card should hold it up when it is said, and all of the children should run in place.

The children with the *kid, lamp,* and *coat* cards should come to the front of the class and stand next to the big book, in the order their words will appear, for the next two lines. As line 11 (**K** is for **kid,** a baby goat) is read, the child who has the *kid* word card should hold it up when the word is said. When line 12 is read (**L** is for **lamp,** but not for coat), the children who have the *lamp* and *coat* word cards should hold them up as they are said.

Before the next two lines are read, the children with the *milk, nut,* and *hat* cards should come to the front of the class and stand next to the big book, in the order their words will appear. As you read these lines, (**M** is for **milk,** cows make that! **N** is for **nut,** but not for hat), the children should hold up their word cards when they are said.

When you read the next two lines of *Alphabet Sounds,* ask the children with the *ox, pup,* and *ring* cards to come to the front of the class and stand next to the big book in the order their words will appear. As you read the first part of line 15 (**O** is for **ox**), the child who has the *ox* word card should hold it up when the word is said. When the second part of line 15 is read (who pulls anything), all of the children should pretend they are pulling something. As you read line 16 (**P** is for **pup,** but not for ring), the children who have the *pup* and *ring* word cards should hold them up as they are said.

The children with the *quit, rake,* and *bat* cards should come to the front of the class and stand next to the big book, in the order their words will appear, for the next two lines. As you read the first part of line 17 (**Q** is for **quit**), the child who has the *quit* word card should hold it up when the word is said. When the second part of line 17 is read (I won't do that!), all of the children should indicate "no" by moving their heads repeatedly from left to right. As you read line 18 (**R** is for **rake,** but not for bat), the children who have the *rake* and *bat* word cards should hold them up as they are said.

The next two lines of *Alphabet Sounds* will involve the children with the *sit, chair, top,* and *bear* cards. They should come to the front of the class and stand next to the big book in the order their words will appear. As the first part of line 19 is read (**S** is for **sit**), the child who has the *sit* word card should hold it up when it is said, and the children should sit down. When the second part of line 19 is read (I love my chair!), the child with the *chair* card should hold it up, and all of the children should put their hands over their hearts and move their bodies to the right and then to the left in a loving fashion. As you read the line 20 (**T** is for **top,** but not for bear), the children who have the *top* and *bear* word cards should hold them up as they are said.

The children with the *us, other, van* and *brother* cards should come to the front of the class and stand next to the big book, in the order their words will appear, before the next two lines are read. As you read the first part of line 21 (**U** is for **us**), the child who has the *us* word card should hold it up when the word is said, and the children should move their hands in a sweeping motion to indicate all of the class members. When the second part of line 21 is read (we love each other!), the child with the *other* card should hold it up when it is said. As you read line 22 (**V** is for **van,** but not for brother), the children who have the *van* and *brother* word cards should hold them up as they are said.

Children with the *wake, bake,* and "ks" cards should come to the front of the class and stand next to the big book. As you read line 23 (**W** is for **wake,** and not for bake), the children who have the *wake* and *bake* word cards should hold them up as they are said. As you read line 24, (**X** is for "**ks,**" a sound fun to make), the child who has the "ks" word card should hold it up when the sound is said, and all of the children should repeat the sound.

For the last two lines of the book, the children with the *you, me, zoo,* and *tree* cards should come to the front of the class and stand next to the big book. As you read line 25 (**Y** is for **you,** and not for me), the children who have the *you* and *me* word cards should hold them up as they are said, and all of the children should point to someone else when the word *you* is said, and point to themselves when the word *me* is said. When the last line is read (**Z** is for **zoo,** but not for tree), the children who have the *zoo* and *tree* word cards should hold them up as they are said.

Matching Words (Word Awareness)

Make separate word cards for all of the letters, words, and punctuation marks used in *Alphabet Sounds*. None of the word cards should have pictures on them since we want the children to rely on each word's letter sequences. Some of the words, such as *is* and *for,* are used in every line at least once. Other words, such as *but* and *not,* are also used frequently. Since this matching activity is done with only two lines of the book at a time, you may want to make only five or six copies of these frequently used words. You will probably want to laminate all of the cards you make, however, so they can be used many times.

Begin the matching activity by distributing to selected children all of the cards containing the letters, words, and punctuation marks used in the first two lines of *Alphabet Sounds*. Ask the children receiving the cards to look at their words, letters, or punctuation marks carefully. Tell them they are going to make the first two lines of the big book by organizing themselves and the cards they have been given in front of the class, so that the letters, words, and punctuation marks are in the same order as they are in the first two sentences of *Alphabet Sounds*.

Display the first two lines of *Alphabet Sounds* and ask the children to read the sentences with you:

> **A** is for **at,** imagine that!

> **B** is for **bug,** but not for cat.

Point to each word as you lead the unison reading of each sentence. Instruct the children with the cards to look at them to see if their word matches any of those in the sentences. Read the two lines again and ask the children with the cards to come to the front of the class and get in the right order to make the two sentences. Help them to get in the right order if they need your help. Three children will have a *for* word card, and two of them will have an *is* card. You may want to tell the children with the *is* and *for* cards which sentences they are to be in, and you may want to tell the children with the two *for* cards in the second sentence which one will appear first and which one will appear second. Help those with the punctuation marks to get in the right order and explain to the children the purpose of these marks. When all of the children are in the right order, the children in their seats should read the sentence as you touch the head of each child representing a letter or word.

Ask the children with the word cards to return them to you and return to their seats. Display the next two lines of *Alphabet Sounds* and help the children read them as before:

C is for **cake,** something good to eat.

D is for **duck,** but not for meat.

Again, distribute letter, punctuation, and word cards to selected students, have them reconstruct the sentences, and have the children in their seats read them as you touch the head of each child holding a letter or word card. Continue this activity with the other pairs of lines in *Alphabet Sounds.*

Children enjoy this matching activity, and by participating in the activity they learn that written words represent spoken words, that letters are used to make words, that spaces in sentences separate individual words, that we read from the left to the right and go from the top of the page to the bottom, and that punctuation marks help us read with expression. Furthermore, some children will also begin to recognize individual words by their letter sequences.

Find the Missing Word

In this activity you will use the word cards you made for the matching activity. In the missing words activity you will use only two lines of the book at a time just as you used in the matching activity.

Begin the missing words activity by distributing to selected children all of the cards containing the letters, words, and punctuation marks used in two of the lines of *Alphabet Sounds.*

Display the two lines of *Alphabet Sounds,* and ask the children to read the sentences with you:

M is for **milk,** cows make that!

N is for **nut,** but not for hat.

Point to each word as you lead the unison reading of each sentence. Instruct the children with the cards to look at them to see if their word matches any of those in the sentences. Read the two lines again, and ask the children with the cards to come to the front of the class and get in the right order to make the two sentences. When all of the children are in the right order, have the children in their seats read the sentences as you touch the head of each child representing a letter or word.

Close the *Alphabet Sounds* big book so the children cannot see the two lines of print from the book, but leave the children in front of the class holding their cards. Ask the children at their seats to close their eyes while you have one of the children in the second line turn his/her card over. The children's sentences are now constructed as follows:

M is for **milk,** cows make that!

N is for _____ , but not for hat.

Point to each word as you lead the unison reading of each sentence. When you come to the missing word, skip over it and continue reading the rest of the words. Ask the children to guess the word that is missing. Once the missing word is identified, it is turned over and read. Continue the activity by hiding various words:

1. **M** is for **milk,** cows make that!

   N is for **nut,** but not for _____ .

2. **M** is for _____ , cows make that!

   N is for **nut,** but not for hat.

3. **M** is for **milk,** _____ make that!

   N is for **nut,** but not for hat.

Once the children have success with the activity, have them guess the missing word without the unison reading of the sentence:

M is for **milk,** cows _____ that!

N is for **nut,** but not for hat.

Eventually, have the children in front of the classroom hide more words than one:

M is for **milk,** cows make _____ !

N is for **nut,** but _____ for hat.

You will probably want to continue this activity with other couplets in _Alphabet Sounds._ Children find the missing words activity enjoyable, and the activity helps them develop word awareness, reading for meaning, making predictions, reading with expression, and print directionality. Furthermore, more children will also begin to recognize individual words by their letter sequences.

Sorting Words According to Number of Letters

You will use the same word cards in the sorting words activity that you used in the word matching and missing words activities. However, you will only need one copy of each unique word used in _Alphabet Sounds: at, and, a, anything, bug, but, baby, bat, bear, brother, bake, cat, cake, cough, curl, coat, cows, chair, duck, don't, do, eat, edge, each, for, fall, fish, fun, good, girl, goat, hair, hat, is, imagine, itch, I, jump, kid, lamp, love, meat, milk, make, my, me, not, nut, off, ox, other, pulls, pup, quit, run, ring, rake, something, squirrel, sit, sound, that, to, that's, top, tree, us, van, who, won't, we, wake, you, zoo._

Begin this activity by distributing all of the word cards to the children in your classroom. Explain to them that they are going to help you organize all of the words in _Alphabet Sounds_ according to how many letters each word has. Write "1" on the chalkboard and have all of the children who have a word made up of only one letter bring it up to the chalkboard. Children should bring up the words *a* and *I*. Put a piece of masking tape on the back of each word and read each one as you stick it onto the chalkboard under the numeral 1.

Next write "2" on the chalkboard and ask the children to find the words that have just two letters in them. Have them brought up to the chalkboard, read them, and stick them onto the chalkboard under the numeral 2. Those words would be: *at, do, is, my, me, ox, to, us,* and *we.*

Continue to sort the words in this fashion until all 74 words are sorted and displayed on the chalkboard:

1	2	3	4	5	7
I	at	and	baby	cough	brother
a	do	bug	bear	chair	imagine
	is	but	bake	other	
	my	bat	cake	pulls	
	me	cat	curl	sound	
	ox	eat	coat	that's	
	to	for	cows		
	us	fun	duck		
	we	hat	don't		
		kid	edge	**8**	**9**
		not	each	anything	something
		nut	fall	squirrel	
		off	fish		
		pup	good		
		run	girl		
		sit	goat		
		top	hair		
		van	itch		
		who	jump		
		you	lamp		
		zoo	love		
			meat		
			milk		
			make		
			quit		
			ring		
			rake		
			that		
			tree		
			won't		
			wake		

Children find the sorting activity interesting, and the activity helps them understand that words can be made of just one letter or, in this example, as many as nine. Research studies reveal that many first grade children believe that all words are made up of the same number of letters—about five or six.

Sorting Words by Initial Letters

The same word cards you used in the previous activity are used in this activity. Begin the activity by distributing all of the word cards to the children in your classroom. Explain to them that they are going to help you organize all of the words in *Alphabet Sounds* according to the first letter in each word. Write "a" on the chalkboard and have all of the children who have a word beginning with the letter *a* bring it up to the chalkboard. Children should bring up the words *at, and, a,* and *anything.* Put a piece of masking tape on the back of these words and stick them onto the chalkboard under the letter *a.*

Next write "b" on the chalkboard and ask the children to find the words that begin with the letter *b.* Have them brought up to the chalkboard and stick them onto the chalkboard under the letter *b.* Those words would be *bug, but, baby, bat, bear, brother,* and *bake.*

Continue to sort the words in this fashion until all 74 words are sorted and displayed on the chalkboard:

a	b	c	d	e	f
at	bug	cat	duck	eat	for
and	but	cake	don't	edge	fall
a	baby	cough	do	each	fish
anything	bat	curl			fun
	bear	coat			
	brother	cows			
	bake	chair*			

g	h	i	j	k	l
good	hair	is	jump	kid	lamp
girl	hat	imagine			love
goat		itch			
		I			

m	n	o	p	q	r
meat	not	off	pull	quit	run
milk	nut	ox	pup		ring
make		other			rake
my					
me					

s	t	u	v	w	y	z
something	that*	us	van	who	you	zoo
squirrel	to			won't		
sit	that's*			we		
sound	top			wake		
	tree					

Note: These words begin with digraphs (*ch, th*), so technically speaking they do not begin with *c* and *t*, but with *ch* and *th*. However, children at this stage of development would not understand this concept so, at this time, when they sort these words according to the first letter of each word, we do not tell them that they are wrong.

This sorting activity focuses children's attention on letters. It develops, or in some cases reinforces, the understanding that words are made of letters. It also helps them recognize that different words can begin with the same letter.

USING BOOKS TO DEVELOP AWARENESS OF RHYME

Explain to children that rhyming words have the same ending sound. Tell them that *tail* and *nail* are rhyming words because they sound alike at the end. Repeat the words *tail* and *nail* again, and ask the children to say them while they listen carefully to the ending sounds of each word. Tell them that *tail* and *cake* are not rhyming words because they do not sound alike at the end. Have the children repeat the words *tail* and *cake.*

As you read *Alphabet Sounds* with the children, ask them to raise their hands when they hear words that rhyme. They will enjoy the activity, and it will help them develop an awareness of rhyme.

Help Children Discriminate Between Rhyming and Nonrhyming Words

Read the first two lines of the big book with the children:

A is for **at,** imagine that!

B is for **bug,** but not for cat.

Ask the children if they can find the rhyming words in the first two lines of *Alphabet Sounds.* If they have difficulty with this task, read the lines again, say the words *that* and *cat,* and help the children see that the ending sounds of the two words are alike. There are also two rhyming words in the first line of the big book. If the children have difficulty perceiving *at* and *that* as rhyming words, help them.

Place some masking tape on the back of the word card **dog** and stick it to the book over the word **cat.** The first two lines of the book now look like this:

> **A** is for **at,** imagine that!
>
> **B** is for **bug,** but not for dog.

Read these lines with the children and ask them if the words *that* and *dog* have the same ending sounds. Remind them that if words do not have the same ending sound, they are not rhyming words. Help the children conclude that the words *that* and *dog* do not rhyme by repeating the two words and asking, "Do the words sound alike at the end? Are the words *that* and *dog* rhyming words?"

Write the following words on the chalkboard:

> **th<u>at</u>**   **th<u>at</u>**
>
> **d<u>og</u>**   **c<u>at</u>**

The rhymes in many of the rhyming words used with young children will be spelled alike. This relationship between "same sounds" and "same spellings" in rhyming words is an important one for young children to perceive. Help the children see that the ending letters of the nonrhyming words are different, while the ending letters of the rhyming words are often the same.

Read the second two lines of the big book with the children, and ask the children if they can find the rhyming words:

> **C** is for **cake,** something good to eat.
>
> **D** is for **duck,** but not for meat.

If the children have difficulty perceiving *eat* and *meat* as rhyming words, read the lines again, repeat the words *eat* and *meat,* and help the children perceive that the two words have the same ending sound.

Place some masking tape on the back of the word card **fish** and stick it to the book over the word **meat.** The second two lines of the book now look like this:

> **C** is for **cake,** something good to eat.
>
> **D** is for **duck,** but not for fish.

Read these lines with the children and ask them if the words *eat* and *fish* have the same ending sounds. Remind them that if words do not have the same ending sounds, they are not rhyming words. Help the children conclude that the words *eat* and *fish* do not rhyme by repeating the two words and asking, "Do the words sound alike at the end? Are the words *eat* and *fish* rhyming words?"

Write the following words on the chalkboard:

<u>eat</u>   <u>eat</u>

<u>fish</u>   m<u>eat</u>

Again, help the children see that the ending letters of the nonrhyming words are different, while the ending letters of the rhyming words are often the same.

Continue this activity with lines 9 and 10, lines 11 and 12, lines 13 and 14, lines 15 and 16, lines 17 and 18, lines 21 and 22, and lines 23 and 24 of the big book. The rhyming words *off* and *cough* in lines 5 and 6, the rhyming words *squirrel* and *curl* in lines 7 and 8, the rhyming words *chair* and *bear* in lines 19 and 20, and the rhyming words *me* and *tree* in lines 25 and 26 are not spelled alike. Therefore, after you have worked with the "same sounds/same spellings" rhymes, introduce children to the "same sounds/different spellings" rhymes, and help them understand that some rhyming sounds are spelled differently. The concept that there are different ways we can spell sounds in words is also an important concept for children to develop.

Creating Rhymes

Begin this activity by reading the first two lines of the big book with the children:

A is for **at,** imagine that!

B is for **bug,** but not for cat.

Now that the children can differentiate between rhyming and nonrhyming words, they are ready to create some rhymes of their own. Use the chalkboard to record the children's work. First, on the chalkboard, copy all of the words of the first two lines of *Alphabet Sounds,* except the last word:

A is for **at,** imagine that!

B is for **bug,** but not for _____ .

Tell the children that you want them to complete the last line by finding another word to rhyme with the word *that.* Ask them to raise their hands if they can think of a word that rhymes with *that.* Record each child's responses on the chalkboard, one at a time, by writing the rhyming word and the name of the child identifying it. For example:

A is for **at,** imagine that!

B is for **bug,** but not for hat.   (Teresa)

Read the revised couplet with the children. Ask them to verify whether Teresa's word does or does not rhyme with the word *that* by helping them decide if the words *that* and *hat* sound alike at the end. Also help them decide if the rhyming parts of *that* and *hat* are spelled alike.

Erase Teresa's rhyme from the chalkboard. Ask for other contributions and repeat the process. Other possible contributions:

> **A** is for **at,** imagine that!
>
> **B** is for **bug,** but not for rat.   (Carlos)

> **A** is for **at,** imagine that!
>
> **B** is for **bug,** but not for fat.   (Tony)

> **A** is for **at,** imagine that!
>
> **B** is for **bug,** but not for pat.   (Michelle)

> **A** is for **at,** imagine that!
>
> **B** is for **bug,** but not for flat.   (Dale)

> **A** is for **at,** imagine that!
>
> **B** is for **bug,** but not for sat.   (Nicole)

> **A** is for **at,** imagine that!
>
> **B** is for **bug,** but not for mat.   (Troy)

If some of the children offer nonrhyming words, accept their contributions just as you would rhyming words (see Phillip's contribution below). Write the child's word at the end of the line, and write the child's name next to the word. Read the revised product and make a positive comment about the contribution. For example, Phillip's word begins like *cat* (the word used in *Alphabet Sounds*), and the last letter of his word is the same as the last letter in the word *that.* Help the children decide, however, if the words *that* and *cut* rhyme by using the same evaluative criteria used with Teresa's contribution.

> **A** is for **at,** imagine that!
>
> **B** is for **bug,** but not for cut.   (Phillip)

DEVELOPING PHONEMIC AWARENESS AND SIMPLE PHONICS KNOWLEDGE

Research studies on phonemic awareness suggest that children develop an awareness of words before they develop an awareness of rhyming within words. It also suggests that they develop an awareness of rhymes before they begin to develop phonemic awareness. In fact, children's awareness of rhymes enables us to help them develop the beginning levels of phonemic awareness. Remember, phonemic awareness is being aware that spoken words are made of phonemes—the basic sound units we use to create spoken words.

The levels of phonemic awareness, in the order children generally develop them, are

1. Identifying simple single-syllable words when they are spoken in phonemes
2. Associating isolated phonemes with the initial sounds of familiar words
3. Isolating the beginning phonemes of familiar words
4. Associating isolated phonemes with the final sounds of familiar words
5. Isolating the ending phonemes of familiar words
6. Associating isolated phonemes with vowel sounds of familiar words
7. Isolating the vowel phonemes in familiar words
8. Isolating all the phonemes in simple single-syllable words
9. Counting phonemes in words
10. Saying words without the initial phoneme
11. Saying words without the final phoneme
12. Saying words by substituting new phonemes for the original ones

Without phonemic awareness, phonics instruction would be meaningless. Phonics knowledge is knowing that the letters in written words represent specific phonemes. Unless children can hear the phonemes in spoken words, they cannot develop phonics knowledge.

Children can develop some phonics knowledge at the same time they are developing phonemic awareness. Children's awareness of rhyme enables us to begin the instruction that helps them with this developmental process. A single-syllable word can be analyzed by its **rime** (the ending part of the word beginning with its vowel) and the letter, or letters, that come before the rime, which is called the **onset.** (Notice that the "rime" spelling is used instead of the "rhyme" spelling when we are referring to a syllable element.) Since young children find it easier to hear the rime component in a syllable before perceiving its onset, you can begin both early phonemic awareness training and simple phonics instruction with rhyming words. By helping children learn to associate the single consonant letters in rhyming words with the consonant phonemes representing them, they begin to develop both phonemic awareness and phonics knowledge.

Key Words and Pictures for Rimes

The 36 key words shown in Figure 2 contain the following rimes: *ack, ag, ail, ain, ake, ale, ame, amp, an, ank, ap, ash, at, ate, ay, eat, ell, en, est, ick, ide, ill, in, ine, ing, ink, ip, it, ock, oke, op, ot, uck, ug, ump,* and *unk.* These key words also contain 18 onsets: *b, c, d, g, h, j, l, m, n, p, r, s, t, v, w, ch, sh,* and *wh.* The 18 onsets and 36 rimes organized in various ways would comprise about 700 words.

Each child should have a copy of the key words and pictures to use for reference purposes. They may want to refer to the pictures from time to time to help them remember the sounds of the rimes and the onsets that precede them.

Using Rhyming Words to Teach Initial Consonant Phonemes and Graphemes

As children participate in the activities and games that follow, they should develop the ability to isolate onset sounds from the rimes (a phonemic awareness task) and associate the onset sounds with the letter/s representing them (a phonics task). They will also learn to associate the sound of rimes with the letters representing them, make words using the onsets and rimes, and create "hink pinks" (example: *fat cat*).

Making Words with Onsets and Rimes.   Begin this activity by making word cards for the following words: *van, can, fan, man, pan, ran, tan.* Draw a line to separate the onset from the rime in each of these words, put some masking tape on the back of each word card, and place them on the chalkboard. For example:

v	an

c	an

f	an

m	an

p	an

r	an

t	an

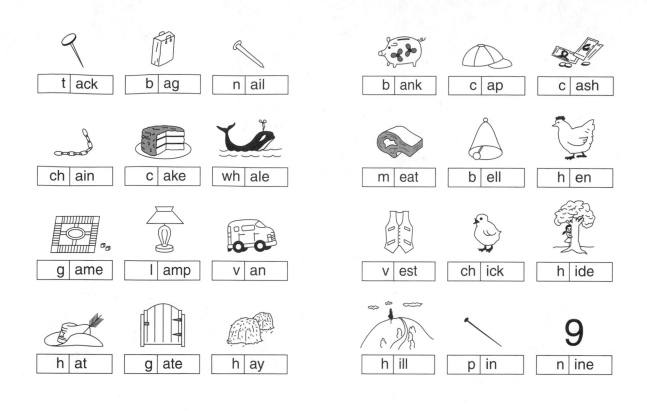

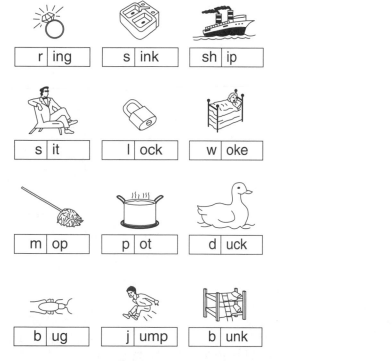

Figure 2

Read the words with the children and ask them to verify whether these words do or do not rhyme with each other. Help them decide if the words sound alike at the end. Help them decide if the rhyming parts of the words are spelled alike.

With a pair of scissors cut the word card *van* into two parts, the onset and the rime. Put masking tape on both parts and place them back on the chalkboard next to each other.

Say the word *van* and ask the children if they can tell you the sound that begins the word. Some of the children will be able to say /v/. Point to the letter *v* and tell them that this is the letter that we use to write that sound. Tell the children that you are going to say the word in two parts, and then say the sounds represented by the onset and the rime as you point to each (/v/ . . . . /an/). Ask the children to say the word in two parts as you point to each part; point to each part and help the children isolate the appropriate sounds.

Next, cut the onsets off the remaining words, put masking tape on each word part, and place all of the word parts back on the chalkboard:

| v | an |

| c | an |

| f | an |

| m | an |

| p | an |

| r | an |

| t | an |

Say each word as you point to it and ask the children to identify its beginning sound. Help them if they need help. After the beginning sound has been identified, point to the letter in the word representing that sound and tell them the name of that letter. Then say the onset and rime and ask the children to say each word part as you point to it. You may want to move the two parts of the word to different places on the chalkboard as you say the parts.

Next, place only one *an* rime on the chalkboard, with all of the onsets in a column next to the rime:

> v
>
> c
>
> f
>
> m   an
>
> p
>
> r
>
> t

This part of the activity gives children the opportunity to isolate the beginning phoneme of a word, select the letter representing the phoneme, and move that letter to the rime to make the word. First, you will say a word (*pan*, for example). The children will tell you what sound is heard at the beginning of the word (/p/). You will reinforce their correct responses, and then you will ask one of the children to come to the chalkboard and move the letter that represents /p/ next to /an/ to make the word *pan*. Repeat this process with all of the other words.

Next, make copies of the *an* rime and the onsets *v, c, f, m, p, r,* and *t.* Give one copy to each group of two students. The rimes and the onsets can be typed onto one piece of paper that the children can cut into separate parts with scissors. Each student team will make words by moving various onsets to the *an* rime as you say each word. All of their work can be reinforced by you, using the large word cards you prepared for the activity.

You may repeat this activity as often as you like, using various rimes and onsets.

Option: You may wish to use a flannelboard rather than a chalkboard for this activity, or any of the other activities in the book that require the use of manipulatives. If so, the manipulatives would need to be prepared to stick on the flannelboard. Magnets and metal boards are also effective if you want to make your manipulatives with magnet sheets.

Making Words Game

This game can be played with two players, two small groups of players, or the entire classroom divided into two groups. The materials needed are two copies of one rime card (*ack,* for example) and cards for all of the single-letter consonants in the alphabet.

Procedures: Each player or team of players is given one of the rime cards. The rime cards are placed face up on the desk or posted on the chalkboard with masking tape. All of the consonant cards are turned face down so they cannot be identified. Each player or team of players randomly picks eight consonant cards, turns them over so they can be identified, and places them in a column on the desk or chalkboard:

Team (or Player) One   **Team (or Player) Two**

b	ack	c	ack
j		r	
l		b	
m		s	
p		d	
r		f	
s		p	
t		j	

Each player should have a copy of the key words and pictures for rimes to help them associate the onsets and rimes with the sounds they represent. The players, or teams, take turns. A child on the first team moves the *b* onset next to the *ack* rime and says the sound represented by the onset followed by the sound represented by the rime (example: "b" . . . "ack"). If the two sounds make a word, the team gets two points. If the two sounds do not make a word, as would be the case with the child on the second team (example: "k" . . . "ack"), but the child says the sounds correctly and correctly acknowledges that a real word has not been made, the team gets one point. Play continues in this fashion until the children have tested all of their onsets and have made as many words as possible.

The players may continue to play the game with the same rime by randomly drawing single-letter onsets again, until they become familiar with the rime. The game may also be continued with other rimes so children can become familiar with them as well. However, this activity is meant to be enjoyed by children rather than forced on them, so let their interests dictate how often and how extensively this activity is pursued.

Later on, after the children have had success with the single-letter onsets, the game may be played with consonant digraph onsets and *qu*. The consonant clusters *th, sh, ch, wh* are called consonant digraphs because each of the two-letter groups represents a single speech sound (actually, you probably remember that the *th* represents two different speech sounds: **_th_**at and **th**ing). You may also remember that the letter *q* doesn't occur without a *u* after it, so when *qu* begins words, it represents the "kw" sound heard in the word *quit*. As the players gain more phonics knowledge, they will also be able to make words with consonant blends. For example, after the word *t ack* has been made by a player, the onset *s* could be placed next to the onset *t* to make another word: *st ack*. **However, at this point in the child's development you should limit the game to the use of single-letter onsets only.**

Creating Hink Pinks.   Begin this activity by making two *at* rime cards, and cards for the following onsets: *b, c, f, h, m, r, s,* and *v*. Put masking tape on the back of each card and place them on the chalkboard in the following manner:

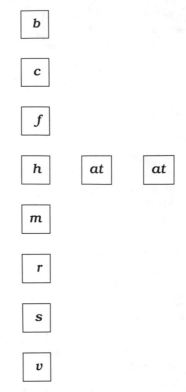

Explain to the children that some rhyming words when they are said together can be used to make funny pictures. Move the *f* onset card next to the first *at* rime, and move the *c* onset card next to the second *at* rime as shown:

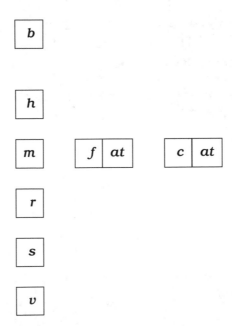

Ask the children to identify the two words you have made. If the children have difficulty identifying the words, help them use the strategy they developed while playing the "Making Words Game." Point to the onset and rime while saying, "/f/ . . . /at/ makes the word _____ ." Repeat this process with the next word, if necessary. After the words have been identified, tell them that you have made a "hink pink." A hink pink is two rhyming words that can be used for drawing funny pictures. Give them the opportunity to write these words on a piece of art paper and draw a picture of a fat cat above the words.

Invite the children to try to create another hink pink using the *at* rime cards and the eight onsets posted on the chalkboard. They might create:

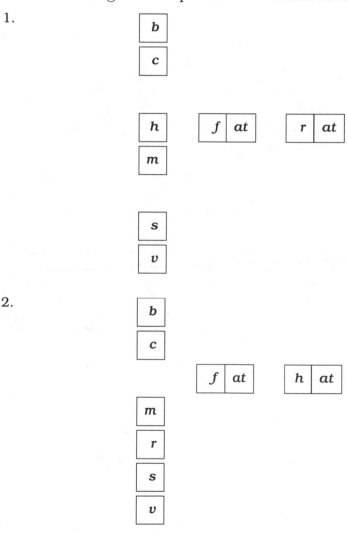

3.

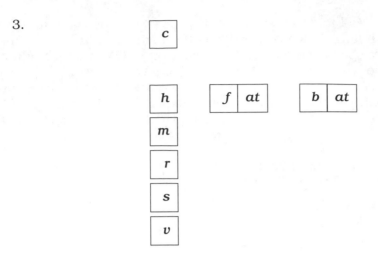

This hink pink activity may be repeated often, using various rimes and onsets.

Hink Pink Game

This game can be played with two players, two small groups of players, or the entire classroom divided into two groups. The materials needed are two sets of cards for all of the single-letter consonant onsets, and two sets of cards for all of the rimes.

Procedures: Each player or team of players is given all of the onset cards. The onset cards are placed in a column in alphabetical order face up on the desk, or posted on the chalkboard with masking tape. One set of rime cards is stacked in a pile face up, and the other set is stacked in a pile face down so they can't be identified. Each player or team of players randomly picks a rime card from the set placed face down and places it face up on the desk, or posts it on the chalkboard. The match for the rime picked is found from the other rime card stack and placed beside it.

Team (or Player) One

b	ake	ake
c		
d		
f		
g		
h		
j		
k		
l		
m		
n		
p		
r		
s		
t		
v		
w		
y		
z		

Team (or Player) Two

b	amp	amp
c		
d		
f		
g		
h		
j		
k		
l		
m		
n		
p		
r		
s		
t		
v		
w		
y		
z		

Each player should have a copy of the key words and pictures for rimes to help them associate the onsets and rimes with the sounds they represent. Both players or teams are given a reasonable amount of time to make a "hink pink" using the rhymes chosen and any of the onsets on the desk or chalkboard. For example, the first player or team might make the hink pink *fake cake,* and the second player or team might make *damp lamp.* Each time a player makes a hink pink within the time allotted, the player gets two points. The game continues by each player or team randomly selecting a new rime. Players may wish to write down the hink pinks they create and illustrate them later.

Matching Consonant Letters and Word Cards

Helping young children learn the sounds associated with single consonant letters is best facilitated by pictures and key words. Copies of the pictures and key words representing common rimes and onsets will be an important reference resource for these children for some time to come. They will help children remember not only consonant letter-sound relationships, but also common rimes in words. Later on, these pictures and key words will help you teach children about consonant digraphs and syllable patterns that indicate to the reader the sounds of the vowels in written words.

The use of written words that rhyme also helps children learn to isolate both the initial consonant phoneme from a spoken rhyme, and the written onset from the written rime so a meaningful association can be made between the consonant phoneme and the letter representing it. The rhyming activities and games presented thus far will be very effective in helping children learn the letters representing consonant phonemes. We are now ready to go back to *Alphabet Sounds* and help children learn to associate each consonant sound with one simple key word.

Alphabet Sounds provides a key word for the 21 consonant letters so that children will have a handy reference to associate the sounds represented by each consonant letter. All of the key words are presented in alphabetical order in the big book, which makes it easy for the children to locate a specific consonant quickly.

This activity helps children master the common sounds represented by consonant letters and helps those who do not master them learn to use *Alphabet Sounds* as a tool to assist them in that task.

Begin this activity by making 20 lowercase letter cards for all of the consonant letters, except *x.* After these cards have been made, have the children sit in a large circle. Distribute the lowercase letter cards to the children. Then distribute to the children 20 uppercase consonant letter cards and the reference word cards for those letters that you made for the matching words activity:

B	bug	C	cake	D	duck		
F	fish	G	girl	H	hair		
J	jump	K	kid	L	lamp		
M	milk	N	nut	P	pup		
Q	quit	R	rake	S	sit		
T	top	V	van	W	wake		
Y	you	Z	zoo				

Some of the children in your classroom will have more than one card. Just make sure that you do not give both the upper- and lowercase letter cards for the same letter, and the matching key word card for that letter, to the same child.

Tell the children that you are going to say the consonant letters that represent the beginning sounds of words, in alphabet order. Tell them that the children having the lower- and uppercase consonant letter cards should hold them up when the appropriate letter is said, and the child having the word card beginning with the sound represented by that letter should also hold up that card. When all three cards are held up, the children should be instructed to say, in unison, the letter name, the letter sound, and the key word. For example, "B . . . /b/ . . . bug."

Using Key Words to Build Word Charts for Beginning Consonant Sounds

If children have difficulty associating consonant letters with the sounds representing them, this activity will be very helpful. Display on the bulletin board the following 18 picture/word cards you made for *Alphabet Sounds: bug, cake, duck, fish, girl, hair, jump, kid, lamp, milk, nut, pup, rake, sit, top, van, wake,* and *zoo.* The bulletin board should be covered with white paper so that the children can write on it. In addition, display on the bulletin board the following letter/word cards for the remaining two consonants representing beginning word sounds: *q, quit* and *y, you.* Each of the picture cards contains the written word and a picture of the word above it. The other two cards will contain only the letter plus the word below it.

bug	cake	duck
ball	cat	dog
boy	come	do
big	car	dig
be	cup	door
by	can	dark

Figure 3 Sample Chart of Words with Identical Beginning Consonant Sounds

The bulletin board will be used to build a chart of words beginning with identical consonant sounds. The children will build the chart. When they find a word they want to add to the chart, they simply write it under the proper key word. A portion of the chart might look like Figure 3.

More Onset and Rime Games

As children participate in the games that follow, they will learn to associate the sound of the rimes with the letters representing them, make words using the onsets and rimes, and sort words according to beginning consonant sounds. Furthermore, they will be exposed to the VCe syllable pattern (*hate*) and the VC syllable pattern (*hat*), which will help readers know when a vowel letter represents its long or short sound. This concept will be learned much later, but the activities that contrast these two patterns will prepare children for this concept when it is developed later on.

Creating Words with Common Rimes. This game can be played with two players, two small groups of players, or the entire classroom divided into two groups. The materials needed are two *t* onset cards, and cards for all of the common rimes: *ack, ag, ail, ain, ake, ale, ame, amp, an, ank, ap, ash, at, ate, ay, eat, ell, en, est, ick, ide, ill, in, ine, ing, ink, ip, it, ock, oke, op, ot, uck, ug, ump,* and *unk.*

Procedures: Each player or team of players is given one of the *t* onset cards. The onset cards are placed on the desk or posted on the chalkboard with masking tape. All of the rhyme cards are turned face down so they cannot be identified. Each player or team of players randomly picks eight rimes, turns them over so they can be identified, and places them on the desk or chalkboard in a column:

Team (or Player) One   **Team (or Player) Two**

t	ap

| ime |
| ail |
| ake |
| en |
| ump |
| op |
| an |

t	ash

| ag |
| ine |
| ank |
| ill |
| ack |
| ap |
| est |

Each player should have a copy of the key words and pictures for rimes to help them associate the onsets and rimes with the sounds they represent. The players or team members take turns. A child on the first team moves the *t* onset next to the *ap* rime and says the sound represented by the onset followed by the sound represented by the rime (example: "t" . . . "ap"). If the two sounds make a word, the team gets two points. If the two sounds do not make a word, as would be the case with the child on the second team (example: "t" . . . "ash"), but the child says the sounds correctly and correctly acknowledges that a real word has not been made, the team gets one point. Play continues in this fashion until the children have tested all of their rimes and have made as many words as possible.

The players may continue to play the game with the same onset by randomly drawing rimes again, or they can use a different onset. Players should be able to play this game with all of the single-letter onsets.

Creating Words with Two Onsets and Common Rimes. This game can be played with two players, two small groups of players, or the entire classroom divided into two groups. The materials needed are two *d* onset cards, two *b* onset cards, and all of the rime cards.

Procedures: Each player or team of players is given a *d* and a *b* onset card. The onset cards are placed on the desk or posted on the chalkboard. Each player or team is given all of the rime cards.

Team (or Player) One   **Team (or Player) Two**

| d | b | | d | b |

Both players or teams are given a reasonable amount of time to (1) place all of the rimes between the two onsets that could be used to make real words with both the onset *d* **and** the onset *b* (for example, the *ump* rime would make the word *dump* with the *d* onset and the word *bump* with the *b* onset); (2) place all of the rimes next to the *d* onset that would make real words with the onset *d*, but not with the onset *b* (for example, *damp*); and (3) place all of the rimes next to the *b* onset that would make real words with the onset *b*, but not with the onset *d* (for example, *bake*).

Example: **Team (or Player) One**

d	amp		ump		b	ake
	ip		ug			at
	ate		ay			eat

     etc.

At the end of the allotted time, the players or teams check each other's work and a point is given for each correct word identified.

Ask each player, or one of the children on each team, to write down each word correctly identified on a separate piece of paper so they can be mixed up, read, and sorted into columns later according to beginning consonant sounds.

For example:

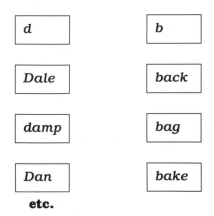

d	b
Dale	back
damp	bag
Dan	bake

     etc.

The game continues by using other single-letter onset pairs. A variation of this game is to allow the players or teams to randomly pick the onset pairs.

Creating Words with Closed and VCe Rimes. This game can be played with two players, two small groups of players, or the entire classroom divided into two groups. The materials needed are two *in* rime cards, two *ine* rime cards, and all of the onset cards except *c, h, j, y,* and *z.*

Procedures: Each player or team of players is given an *in* rime card and a *ine* rime card. The rime cards are placed on the desk or posted on the chalkboard. Each player or team is given all of the onset cards except the ones excluded.

Team (or Player) One   **Team (or Player)Two**

| in | | ine | | in | | ine |

Both players or teams are given a reasonable amount of time to (1) place all of the onsets between the two rimes that could be used to make real words with both the rime *in* **and** the rime *ine* (for example, the *f* onset would make the word *fin* with the *in* rime and the word *fine* with the *ine* rime); (2) place all of the onsets next to the *in* rime that would make real words with the rime *in*, but not with the rime *ine* (for example, *bin*); and (3) place all of the onsets next to the *ine* rime that would make real words with the *ine* rime but not with the *in* rime (for example, *line*).

Example: **Team (or Player) One**

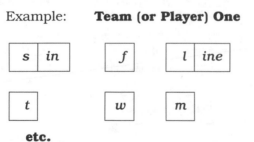

etc.

At the end of the allotted time, the players or teams check each other's work and a point is given for each correct word identified.

Ask each player, or one of the children on each team, to write down each word correctly identified on a separate piece of paper so they can be mixed up, read, and sorted into columns later according to rimes. For example:

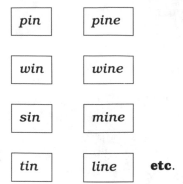

When children see the words in separate rime lists, some of them may discover that the vowel sounds in the words ending with a consonant (*in*) represent the short vowel sound, and the vowel sounds in the words ending with a consonant and an *e* (*ine*) represent the long sound of the vowel. This is an important phonics pattern for children to discover. However, if they do not make the discovery, do not force the issue at this stage of development.

Later on, children may discover that they can combine single-letter onsets to make words beginning with consonant blends (examples: *grin, brine, spin, spine, swine, twin, twine, shrine*). However, at this stage of development, that probably won't happen.

You may continue this game by using the rimes *at* and *ate* and the rimes *ack* and *ake*. With the first pair of rimes, use all of the onsets except *j, k, n, w, y,* and *z*. With the second pair of rimes, use all of the onsets except *d, g, k, n, v, y,* and *z*.

Again, you will want the children to write down all of the words correctly identified on a separate piece of paper so they can be mixed up, read, and sorted into columns according to the rhyme pattern. For example:

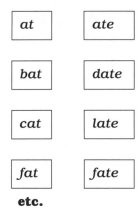

Making Words with Ending Consonant Graphemes

Phonics instruction for children is meaningless without phonemic awareness. Therefore, beginning phonics instruction should follow children's phonemic awareness development. You have probably noticed that the activities and games presented thus far have been organized around children's developmental stages of phonemic awareness.

Developmentally speaking, children are able to hear rhyming words before they are able to hear beginning consonant phonemes in words. They are also able to hear single-consonant phonemes at the beginning of words before they are able to hear single-consonant phonemes at the end of words. Furthermore, they are able to hear single final consonant phonemes at the end of words before they are able to hear vowel phonemes in the medial position of words.

Activities focused on words' final phonemes, although challenging to some, are appropriate for children who can hear words' initial consonant phonemes and identify the letters representing them. Therefore, final consonant phoneme segmentation, and letter association with the phonemes isolated, is the next area of focus. Begin your final consonant instruction by making word cards for the following words: *bug, bus, but, bud, bun, buzz, buck.* Draw a line to separate the final consonant grapheme from the rest of the word, put some masking tape on the back of each word card, and place them on the chalkboard.

For example:

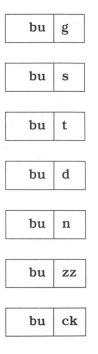

Read the words for the children. Then say each word again in two parts. The first part is the beginning consonant phoneme coarticulated with the vowel sound, and the second part is the ending consonant phoneme. For example, /bu/ . . . /g/; /bu/ . . . /s/; /bu/ . . . /t/; etc. Ask the children to verify whether these words do or do not sound alike at the beginning. Help the children decide if the beginning parts of the words are spelled alike.

With a pair of scissors cut the word card *bug* into two parts: the consonant-vowel and the ending consonant. Put masking tape on both parts and place them on the chalkboard next to each other.

bu	g

Say the word *bug* and ask the children to tell you the sound they hear at the end of the word *bug*. Repeat the sound (/g/). Point to the letter *g* and tell them that *g* is the letter used to write that sound. Tell the children that you are going to say the word in two parts. Then say the sounds represented by the letters in the first part of the word followed by the ending consonant, and point to each part as you say it (example, /bu/ . . . /g/). Ask the children to say the word in two parts as you point to each part; point to each part and help the children isolate the appropriate sounds.

Next, cut the ending consonants off the remaining words, put masking tape on each word part, and place all of the word parts back on the chalkboard:

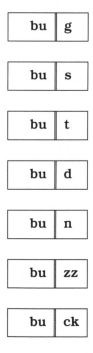

Say each word individually as you point to it (example, *bug*). Ask the children if they can identify the ending sound of the word (example /g/). Help them if they need help. After the ending sound has been identified, point to the letter, or letters, in the word representing that sound and tell them the name of the letter/s. Then say the word in two parts and ask the children to repeat each word part as you point to it. You may want to move the two parts of the word to different places on the chalkboard as you say the parts.

Next, place only one *bu* card on the chalkboard, with all of the final consonant graphemes in a column next to the *bu* card:

g

s

t

bu   d

n

zz

ck

This activity gives children the opportunity to isolate the ending phoneme of a word; select the letter, or letters, representing the phoneme; and move the letter/s to the beginning consonant-vowel to make the word. First, you will say a word (*bus*, for example). The children will tell you what sound is heard at the ending of the word (/s/). You will reinforce their correct responses, and then you will ask one of the children to come to the chalkboard and move the letter that represents /s/ next to /bu/ to make the word *bus*. Repeat this process with all of the other words.

Next, make copies of the *bu* card and the consonant graphemes *g, s, t, d, n, zz,* and *ck*. Give one copy to each group of two students. The word parts can be typed onto one piece of paper that the children can cut into separate parts with scissors. Each student team will make words by moving various consonant graphemes to the *bu* part as you say each word. You can reinforce all of their work using the large word cards you prepared for the activity.

You may repeat this activity as often as you like, using word beginnings and final consonant graphemes.

Using Key Words to Build Word Charts for Ending Consonant Sounds

Key word pictures are helpful in building word charts for ending consonant sounds, just as they were in building word charts for initial consonant phonemes. Display on the bulletin board the following 15 picture/word cards: *tub, kid, roof, bug, cage, duck, girl, gum, van, pup, us, hat, five, ox,* and *fuzz.* You have already made many of these word cards for previous activities. The new picture/word cards to make are *tub, roof, cage, gum, five,* and *fuzz.* You may elect to cut pictures from books or magazines, rather than draw them. However, the pictures with the word cards help young children remember the sounds that are represented by the ending consonant letters.

Incidentally, the grapheme representing /j/ at the end of words is spelled *ge,* so the word *cage* is the key word representing that ending consonant phoneme. When the letter *v* occurs at the end of words, it always has an *e* after it, so the word *five* is the key word for the ending phoneme /v/. Furthermore, because an *e* is written after consonant letters in VCe patterned syllables to indicate that the vowels in those syllables are long, many of the other ending consonant sounds will be spelled with an *e* after the consonant (*tube, hate, ride*) or without the *e* (*tub, hat, rid*).

The 15 key picture/word cards are displayed on a bulletin board covered with white paper so the children can write their words ending with consonant sounds under the appropriate picture/word card. Some of the spellings of the words written under a picture/word card will be different because of the various ways we spell ending consonant sounds. However, since this is a chart of words with common consonant endings, this poses no problem. In fact, it helps children become aware of an important "concept of print." A portion of the chart might look like Figure 4.

Using Key Words to Teach Short Vowel Sounds

Becoming aware of vowel phonemes in the medial position of words is difficult for very young children. Therefore, helping them learn to hear the vowel sounds in words is best facilitated by presenting them in the initial position of simple single-syllable words. The key vowel words in *Alphabet Sounds* were chosen with this in mind.

Alphabet Sounds provides a key word for the five vowel letters when those letters represent short vowel sounds. Short vowel sounds are used

Figure 4 Sample Chart of Words with Identical Ending Consonant Sounds

more frequently in words than any other sounds. These five key words give children something they can use to associate the short vowel sounds with the letters representing them.

Begin this activity by making five word cards for the five short vowel key words presented in *Alphabet Sounds*. Cut the words apart after the vowel, put masking tape on each word part, and place the word parts on the chalkboard:

a	t

e	dge

i	tch

o	x

u	s

Say each word as you point to it (example: *at*). Say each word part as you point to it (example: /a/ . . . /t/). Ask the children if they can identify the beginning sound of the word (example: /a/). Help them if they need help. After the beginning sound has been identified, point to the letter in the word representing that sound and tell them the name of the letter (*a*). Then say the word in two parts and ask the children to repeat each word part as you point to it. You may want to move the two parts of the word to different places on the chalkboard as you say the parts.

Matching Vowel Letters and Word Cards

Make five lowercase letter cards for all of the five vowels. After these cards have been made, have the children sit in a large circle. Distribute the lowercase letter cards to the children. Then distribute five uppercase vowel letter cards, and the reference word cards for those letters, that you made for the matching words activity. Those cards are:

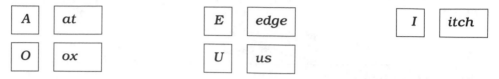

When you distribute the ten letter cards and the five word cards, make sure you do not give more than one card to a student.

Begin the activity with the *Alphabet Sounds* big book. Read with the children the lines that present the vowel letters. Leave the big book open so the children can refer to it, if needed. Tell the children that you are going to say the vowel letters that represent the vowel sounds in words, in alphabetical order. Tell them that the children having the lower- and uppercase vowel letter cards should hold them up when the appropriate letter is said, and the child having the word card beginning with the vowel sound represented by that letter should also hold up that card. When all three cards are held up, the children should be instructed to say in unison the letter name, the letter sound, and the key word (for example, "A . . . /a/ . . . at").

Using Key Words to Build Word Charts for Vowel Sounds

Make five letter cards for all of the five vowel letters. Display them on a bulletin board covered with white paper. Also display the five key word cards for short vowel sounds. Explain to the children that each vowel letter represents two sounds. Tell them that the sounds most frequently represented by the vowel letters are the sounds represented by the key words. Point to the key words on the bulletin board. Tell them that the other sound represented by the vowel letters is the sound we hear when we say the name of the vowel letter. Point to the letter cards on the bulletin board.

Explain to the children that they will use this bulletin board to write words containing long and short vowel sounds. When they find a word they want to add to the chart, they simply write it under the proper key word or letter. A portion of the chart might look like Figure 5.

Building a word chart for vowel sounds helps children discover that there are different ways to spell vowel sounds. This concept helps prepare children for later instruction regarding vowel team patterns and syllable patterns that are used to help the reader know when vowel letters represent long and short vowel sounds.

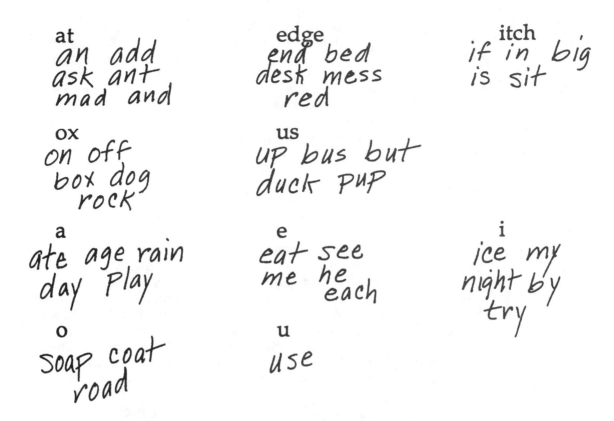

Figure 5 Sample Word Chart for Vowel Sounds

EARLY WRITING ACTIVITIES

Children should be given opportunities to write as soon as they become aware of the written language in their environment. There are many ways to help children become phonemically aware, but perhaps none are as effective as writing, especially when that writing involves invented spelling.

The earliest writing experiences provided for children might be those associated with the Language Experience Approach (LEA) to reading. This approach has been used effectively in classrooms for years. When teachers and children share common experiences in the classroom or on field trips, they discuss these experiences and write about them. Children provide the content for the written products produced. Teachers simply write down what children say while the children watch them do it. Teachers repeat each word a child says while writing it down. Afterwards, the teacher and the children read what was said. Sometimes children copy down the written product so they can read it to others.

Many benefits are associated with using the LEA to introduce children to both reading and writing. First, the written products resulting from this approach contain children's sentence patterns and their vocabulary. Children often find it difficult to understand the syntax and vocabulary of adults. By controlling these two variables when introducing children to their first reading experiences, they are able to focus on the critical aspects of print without being distracted by unfamiliar syntax and vocabulary. Second, children begin to realize that what they can say can be written and read. They conceptualize that speaking, listening, reading, and writing are related, and that they are all important components of our oral and written communication system. Third, through the LEA, children can be introduced to the process writers use as they write, a process that begins with getting ideas for writing, followed by getting those ideas written down, followed by revising and reorganizing those ideas, followed by editing the written work, and ending with sharing or publishing the written work. Finally, the LEA provides a natural bridge to independent writing. An outcome generally associated with effective LEA activities is that children develop an increased interest in producing their own written products using whatever skills and tools they have acquired, no matter how limited they might be.

I would recommend that you introduce children to writing early; that you use the LEA frequently, helping children record experiences important to them; and that you encourage children to do independent writing early, regardless of their level of literacy development.

Writing Alphabet Books

In addition to the other writing activities used in the classroom, you might want to rewrite *Alphabet Sounds* with the children. This activity will help children continue to develop their early phonics knowledge, involve them in writing, and give them an opportunity to be creative. Use the LEA as the writing vehicle for this activity. Begin by writing the first two lines of *Alphabet Sounds* on the chalkboard:

> **A** is for **at,** imagine that!
>
> **B** is for **bug,** but not for cat.

Read the lines with the children. Invite them to come up with a different word for the word *at*. Tell them that the word they choose must begin with the /a/ sound. Various children might suggest words such as *apple, am, add,* etc. Ask the group to vote on the word they like best. After they have decided on the word, erase the word *at* and write the word selected by the children in its place:

> **A** is for **apple,** imagine that!
>
> **B** is for **bug,** but not for cat.

Read the revised version with the children. Next ask them to identify a different word for the word *bug* in the second line. Ask them to tell you what sound the new word must have at the beginning. Repeat the process you followed previously as you help the children select their replacement for the word *bug.* The revised version might be:

> **A** is for **apple,** imagine that!
>
> **B** is for **boy,** but not for cat.

Continue this process with all of the other lines in *Alphabet Sounds.* After the revised version of *Alphabet Sounds* has been written, the children should have the opportunity to copy the new version so they can read it to their parents or some other person. This gives them an opportunity to practice their manuscript handwriting.

Early Spelling Experiences

As children continue to develop phonemic awareness and early phonics knowledge, give them opportunities to engage in simple spelling activities. Spelling instruction should also be organized around children's phonemic awareness development. First, give children the opportunity to spell initial consonant sounds. For example, you might give the children a copy of the following and ask them to spell the words you say by writing in the missing letters:

	an

	an

	an

	an

	an

	an

	an

Say, "Spell the word *van*." "Spell the word *fan*." "Spell the word *can*." "Spell the word *man*." "Spell the word *pan*." "Spell the word *ran*." "Spell the word *tan*."

Second, give children an opportunity to spell ending consonant sounds. For example, you might give children a copy of the following and ask them to spell the words you say by writing in the missing letters:

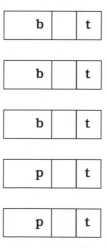

Say, "Spell the word *bug*." "Spell the word *but*." "Spell the word *bun*." "Spell the word *bus*." "Spell the word *bud*."

Finally, give children an opportunity to spell medial vowel sounds. For example, you might give children a copy of the following and ask them to spell the words you say by writing in the missing letters:

Say, "Spell the word *bat*." "Spell the word *but*." "Spell the word *bet*." "Spell the word *bit*." "Spell the word *pot*." "Spell the word *pet*."

Using Key Words to Write Other Words

A final writing activity focuses on helping children use their invented spelling abilities as they write. Begin this activity by displaying all of the key word cards used in *Alphabet Sounds: at, bug, cake, dog, edge, fish, girl, hair, itch, jump, kid, lamp, milk, nut, ox, pup, quit, rake, sit, top, us, van, wake, you,* and *zoo.* The pictures you made or cut out of books/magazines should be included in this display so that children can locate a picture for easy letter-sound reference when memory fails them.

Display the first two word cards:

a	t

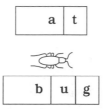

b	u	g

Tell the children that you are going to have them write words according to their sounds. Tell them that all of the sounds in the words you want them to write are represented by the letters in these two words. Tell them that you want them to write the word *but* first. After you say the word, isolate all of the sounds in the word for the children: /b/ . . . /u/ . . . /t/. For children who need help, tell them that the first thing they need to do is write the letter representing /b/. Tell them to look at the first two word cards for that letter. Then ask them to write the letter representing /u/ next to the first letter. Again, tell them to look at the first two word cards for that letter. Then ask them to write the letter representing /t/ next to the second letter.

Have them write other words using the sounds represented by letters in these two words, such as *tag, bat, tug, gag,* and so on. Continue this activity with other word cards. The activity will help children develop the confidence they need to engage in independent writing. However, do not spend a lot of time (no more than 10 minutes) in one sitting on this activity. Short daily mini-lessons on writing words by sounds are better than longer, sporadic lessons.

Explain to the children that they can write almost any word that they can say if they can hear the separate sounds (phonemes) in the word they want to write, and if they can write letters representing all of those sounds. Explain to them that all of their words will not be spelled the way that adults spell them, but learning the correct spelling of words is something that occurs over time. Also explain to them that the ability to write is so important that they need to start writing even before they know how to spell all of the words they write. Help them understand that their writing experiences will help them learn to be better writers and spellers. Help them also understand that the things they have to write about are more important right now than their spelling abilities.

Chapter 8

Learning to Read and Write Single-Syllable Words

Probably the most important keys to learning to read and write single-syllable words are (1) the syllable patterns used to help readers know when single vowel letters represent long or short vowel sounds, and (2) the vowel team patterns used to help readers know which vowel phoneme the vowel team represents. If we add to this important knowledge an understanding of consonant clusters (digraphs and blends), our abilities to write and read single-syllable words increase.

Syllable Patterns

To say that phonics is the association of graphemes with phonemes is simplistic. Yet, this seems to be the popular definition of phonics among reading teachers. Realistically speaking, phonics is much more than a simple association between the graphemes in written words and the phonemes in spoken words. Because there are only five vowel letters in the written American English language system, and these five vowel letters must be used in some way to represent 19 vowel phonemes in the American English oral language system, some means had to be devised so the vowel letters could predictably represent more than one sound. One of the ways our written language system accomplishes this is by the written form of the syllable.

Remember, we have described the syllable as the smallest pronunciation unit of our spoken language, and we have defined the syllable as the smallest part of the spoken word that contains one vowel sound. The way we write these pronunciation units informs readers about the sounds represented by the vowel letters. If we write a syllable this way: *mad,* the vowel letter represents a different sound than if we write the syllable this way: *made.* However, the number of phonemes in each of these words is the same; that is, when we say *mad* and *made,* they both contain three speech sounds (phonemes). Moreover, the initial and final consonant phonemes in each of these words are the same. In sum, the only difference in the words *mad* and *made*, when we say them, is the sound of the vowel phoneme. The letter *e* added at the end of the word *made* is one of the ways our written language system helps us realize that the vowel letter in that word represents its long sound. This syllable pattern has been called the VCe syllable pattern because the vowel letter is followed by one consonant letter and the letter *e*.

When we speak of pronunciation units (the syllables), those units either end in a vowel phoneme (for example: **me, so, ba** con, **ti** ger, **mu** sic) or a consonant phoneme (for example: **men, sod, bat, tip, mud,** or **eve, bone, bake, mine, fuse**). We call syllables ending in vowel phonemes open syllables, and the vowel phonemes in open syllables are generally long. When those syllables are written, they end in vowel letters; therefore, the syllable pattern helps us predict the vowel phoneme sound. However, when we speak syllables ending in consonant phonemes, the vowel phonemes can be either long or short (**sob, stone**). Therefore, we call written syllables ending in consonant phonemes closed syllables if there isn't an *e* after the single consonant, and VCe syllables if the letter *e* is written after the single consonant letter.

In summary then, vowel letters in open syllables (*me, so*) and VCe syllables (*mine, bake*) predictably represent long vowel sounds. Vowel letters in closed syllables (*end, cat, scratch, inch*) predictably represent short vowel sounds.

Vowel Team Patterns

A fourth syllable pattern is the vowel team syllable. These syllables contain vowel teams (*beach, bird, coin, boy, seen*). However, it is the vowel team pattern itself that predicts the vowel phoneme it represents. We have a vowel team when a vowel letter is teamed with another letter to represent a vowel phoneme. Sometimes the letter teamed with the vowel letter is another vowel letter (**soa**p). At other times the vowel letter is teamed with the letter *y, w,* or *r* (**may, cow, bur**st).

The activities presented in this unit are designed to help children (1) discover the syllable patterns that reliably predict vowel phonemes; (2) discover the vowel team patterns that reliably predict vowel phonemes; (3) learn to coarticulate single consonant phonemes at the beginning of words with the vowel phonemes following them; (4) discover the difference between consonant digraphs and consonant blends; and (5) learn to coarticulate consonant clusters (digraphs and blends) at the beginning of words with the vowel phonemes following them. All of the activities are focused on helping children learn to read and write words of one syllable.

DISCOVERING SYLLABLE PATTERNS

Write the following words on the chalkboard before beginning this discovery activity:

1	2	3	Key
go	fin	fine	italic letters (blue) = short vowel sound
he	dim	dime	boldface letters (green) = long vowel sound
so	rid	ride	underlined letters (red) = silent
she	rip	ripe	
we	rob	robe	
be	hop	hope	
me	hid	hide	
no	not	note	
lo	tap	tape	
ye	cut	cute	

Before beginning this activity, review the concept of a syllable with the children. Help them understand that a syllable is a word or part of a word containing one vowel sound. Explain to them that there are four basic ways we write syllables and the lists of words on the chalkboard represent three of them. Tell the children that all of the words you have written on the chalkboard have only one vowel sound. Although the words in column three have two vowel letters, the underlined *e* in each word does not represent a sound.

Tell them that you are going to read the words in each column with them. Ask them to listen carefully to the vowel sounds in each word as the words are read. Read the words in column 1 with the children, and when you have finished, ask the children to tell you whether the vowel sounds in those words are long or short. After they have responded correctly, write "long" above the first word in that column. Repeat this process with the words in both of the other columns. When you are finished, you should have the words "long" written above the first words in columns 1 and 3, and "short" written above the first word in column 2.

Ask the children to carefully study the words in columns 1 and 2 to see if they can discover how the words in those columns differ from each other. If the children have difficulty seeing the difference, ask them to look at the endings of the words in both columns. If they still have difficulty, ask them if the words in column 1 end in a vowel or a consonant. Then ask them if the words in column 2 end in a vowel or a consonant. These questions should help them conclude that the words in column 1 end in vowels, and the words in column 2 end in consonants.

After the children have perceived the difference between the words in column 1 and column 2, ask them to write a statement that would describe why the vowels in the words of the first column represent the long vowel sound, while the vowels in the words of the second column represent the short vowel sound. Their statements should reflect this generalization: **The vowel letters in syllables ending with vowels usually represent their long sounds, and the vowel letters in syllables ending with consonants usually represent their short sounds.**

Ask the children to carefully study the words in columns 2 and 3 to see if they can discover how those words differ. Again, if they have difficulty, ask them to look at the endings of the words in both columns. They should conclude that the words in column 2 end in consonants and the words in column 3 end in consonants followed by an *e*.

Once again, after the children have perceived the difference between the words in columns 2 and 3, ask them to write a statement that would describe why the vowels in the words in column 3 represent their long sounds. Their statements should reflect this generalization: **The vowel letters in syllables ending with one consonant followed by an *e* usually represent their long sounds.**

Help the children conclude that vowel letters represent their long sounds when they are in syllables ending with a vowel *and* when they are in syllables ending with one consonant followed by an *e*. Vowel letters represent their short sounds when they are in syllables ending in consonants.

SYLLABLE PATTERN ACTIVITY WITH SINGLE CONSONANTS

Prepare cards for the following phonics elements. Make them large enough for all of the children in the classroom to see, put masking tape on the back of each element, and stick each element on the chalkboard.

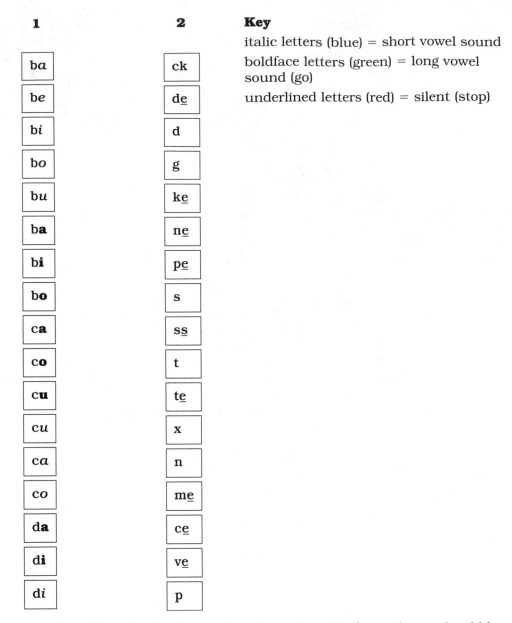

1	2	Key
		italic letters (blue) = short vowel sound
b*a*	ck	boldface letters (green) = long vowel sound (go)
be	d<u>e</u>	underlined letters (red) = silent (stop)
b*i*	d	
bo	g	
b*u*	k<u>e</u>	
ba	n<u>e</u>	
b**i**	p<u>e</u>	
b**o**	s	
ca	s<u>s</u>	
co	t	
c**u**	t<u>e</u>	
c*u*	x	
c*a*	n	
c*o*	m<u>e</u>	
d**a**	c<u>e</u>	
d*i*	v<u>e</u>	
d*i*	p	

Note: The vowel letters in the elements in the first column should be colored blue or green. All of the vowel letters italicized in the columns represent blue, and those bolded represent green. The vowel letters in the elements in the second column are colored red. The underlined vowel letters in the second column represent red. (You may want to underline the letters with either a blue, green, or red magic marker instead of writing the letters in those colors.) Green means "go" and red means "stop." Green suggests that children go ahead and say the letter's name (long sound), and red suggests they stop and not say anything. Vowel letters in blue represent their short sounds.

Procedures: Divide the class into dyad groups (a dyad group is a group of two students). The children in each group should have pencils and paper. They should be instructed to make two column headings on their papers: "1. Long Vowel Words" and "2. Short Vowel Words." The words they construct should be written under the appropriate column headings.

Instructions to the children: "Today we are going to see how many words we can read and write by taking word parts from the first column and combining them with word parts from the second column. The word parts in column 1 are the beginnings of words and the word parts in column 2 are the endings of words. All of the vowel letters underlined in blue in column 1 represent short vowel sounds. All of the vowel letters underlined in green in column 1 represent long vowel sounds. All of the vowel letters in red in column 2 do not represent any sound at all.

"Look at the first word beginning in column 1. The vowel represents /a/. The consonant and the vowel together represent /ba/. To make a word, I look for an ending in column 2 to go with /ba/. Since my vowel sound is short, I will look for an ending that ends in a consonant, rather than an ending that ends in a consonant followed by an *e.* [**Take the** *ba* **beginning off the board and post it next to the** *ck* **ending.**] The first ending in column 2 represents /k/. Those parts would go together to make the word /ba/ . . . /k/, and the letters *b-a-ck* correctly spell the word *back.* I will write that word on my paper under the heading 'Short Vowel Words.'

"Look at the sixth word beginning in column 1. The vowel represents /ā/. The consonant and the vowel together represent /bā/. To make a word, I look for an ending in column 2 to go with /bā/. Since my vowel sound is long, I will look for an ending that ends in a consonant followed by an *e,* rather than a consonant without an *e.* [**Take the** *ba* **beginning off the board and post it next to the** *ke* **ending.**] The fifth ending in column 2 represents /k/. Those parts would go together to make the word /bā/ . . . /k/, and the letters *b-a-ke* correctly spell the word *bake.* I will write that word on my paper under the heading 'Long Vowel Words.'

"Now I am going to give you _____ minutes (set a reasonable time limit) to see how many words you can make and spell correctly. At the end of our time, we will see which team has identified the most words. At this time each team should check with a dictionary to make sure all of the words identified are spelled correctly. You may begin now."

Option: You may elect to modify this activity by having the students copy the word parts on paper squares so they can actually move the word beginnings to the word endings as they experiment with the various combinations that make words.

This activity gives children the practice they need in blending single consonant phonemes with vowels, and with blending consonant endings to those units. They get this practice **without distorting phonemes.** For example, they do not pronounce *ba*, /bu/-/a/, but /ba/, and they do not blend the words' phonemes /bu/-/ak/, but /ba/-/k/. This activity also focuses children's attention on how the syllable pattern informs readers and writers about the sound of the vowel letter. Furthermore, since the activity is gamelike, challenging, and competitive, it keeps children involved long enough for this concept to take root. The activity also improves children's spelling. It helps those children who are in the alphabetic phase of decoding and spelling to begin the move into the orthographic phase.

Incidentally, the word parts in this activity can be used to make at least 64 words. I include only a portion of the words here so you can see how a child's paper might look at the conclusion of the activity:

1. Long Vowel Words	2. Short Vowel Words
bake	back
bike	bad
bite	bag
bone	bat
cake	bed
cane	beg
code	bet
coke	big
cone	bit
cove	boss
cute	cut
date	dig
dime	did
dive	dig

There were only three beginning consonants used in this activity—the first three consonants of the alphabet. This activity may be repeated with all, or some, of the other consonants. There is value in giving children experience blending the other consonants with long and short vowel sounds. Their phonics knowledge grows, their spelling improves, and their word recognition is enhanced.

DISCOVERING CONSONANT DIGRAPHS

Write the following words on the chalkboard before beginning this discovery activity:

1	**2**	**3**	**4**	**5**
ch	sh	wh	th	<u>th</u>
chop	shut	whip	thin	that
chin	ship	when	thick	than
chase	shake	which	thud	them
choke	shame	whale	thug	these

Explain to the children that when we have two consonant letters representing one sound we call those letters a digraph. Call their attention to the letters *ch, sh, wh,* and *th* at the top of each column and explain to them that these are digraphs because the two letters represent only one sound.

Tell the children that you are going to read the words in each column with them. Ask them to listen carefully to the beginning sounds in each word as the words are read. Read the words in column 1 with the children, and when you have finished, ask them to tell you the sound represented by the letters *ch.* Repeat this process with *sh* and *wh.* Help them understand that the beginning sound of *wh* is /hw/ and not /w/; the /hw/ sound is voiceless while the /w/ phoneme is voiced.

Read the words in columns 4 and 5 with the children before you ask them about the two sounds represented by the digraph *th.* After you have read the words in both columns, ask the children if they can tell you the difference between the sounds represented by *th* in the words in columns 4 and 5. After they have identified the difference, help them perceive that the sound represented by the digraph *th* in the words in column 4 is voiceless (we do not use our voice when we make the sound), while the sound represented by that digraph in the words in column 5 is voiced (we use our voice to make the sound). Tell them that you have underlined the digraph that represents the voiced sound to distinguish it from the one representing the voiceless sound. Ask the children to touch their throats with a hand while they say the sounds of /th/ and /*th*/. They will feel a vibration on their hands when they say /<u>th</u>/, but they will feel no vibration when they say /th/.

Refer them to the key words and pictures for rimes and ask them to locate the key words representing the digraphs *wh, ch,* and *sh.* They should locate the key words *whale, chain* (or *chick*), and *ship* and their corresponding pictures. Ask them to choose two familiar words they can use as reference words to help them remember the two sounds represented by the digraph *th.*

SYLLABLE PATTERN ACTIVITY WITH BEGINNING CONSONANT DIGRAPHS

The cards needed for the consonant digraphs activity are listed below:

1	2	Key
cha	s<u>e</u>	italic letters (blue) = short vowel sound
che	s<u>e</u>	boldface letters (green) = long vowel sound (go)
chi	p	underlined letters (red) = silent (stop)
cho	ck	
ch**a**	n	
chi	m<u>e</u>	
ch**o**	k<u>e</u>	
sh**a**	d<u>e</u>	
shi	p<u>e</u>	
sha	v<u>e</u>	
shu	n<u>e</u>	
sho	l<u>e</u>	
wh**a**	t<u>e</u>	
whi	s	
whi	m	
whe	g	
<u>th</u>a	t	
<u>th</u>e	<u>ss</u>	
<u>th</u>**e**		
thi		
thu		

Procedures: Divide the class into dyad groups and give pencils and paper to the children in each group. Ask the children to make two column headings on their papers: 1. "Long Vowel Words" and 2. "Short Vowel Words." The words they construct should be written under the appropriate column headings.

Instructions to the children: The instructions for this activity are similar to those you used with the single consonant letters, except that since you are working with consonant digraphs, you will need to give some additional explanations regarding the pronunciation key for word parts. The underlined <u>th</u> represents the voiced sound of that digraph (*the*), and the *th*, not underlined, represents the voiceless sound (*thing*). You may also have noticed that one of the s's in s<u>e</u> is italicized in the word endings column and the other is not. The italicized *s* represents /z/, and the *s* not italicized represents /s/.

Children should be encouraged to say the vowel sound in the beginning word part first and then coarticulate the digraph with the vowel sound to get the correct pronunciation of the beginning word element. Then they should search the word ending column for suitable endings—either an ending with a consonant, if the vowel sound is short, or an ending with a consonant followed by an *e*, if the vowel sound is long.

The dyad groups should be given a reasonable amount of time to make their word lists, and the competition between the dyad groups should be friendly and fun. At the end of the allotted time, each team should check with a dictionary to make sure all of the words they identified are spelled correctly.

In addition to the benefits of this type of activity already mentioned, this particular activity with digraphs might help children resolve a problem common to many regarding the phonemes represented by *w* and *wh*. In fact, you might want to talk about these phonemes before children participate in the digraph activity. The word *whip* should be pronounced /hwip/ rather than /wip/ as many people pronounce it. In the speech patterns of many people, the phonemes represented by the digraph *wh* and consonant letter *w* are the same, rather than different. Therefore, some of the children may try to make the word *wipe* from whi + pe or the word *wise* from whi + s<u>e</u>. As children make mistakes of this type, you can use those mistakes to provide them with a learning experience they will not likely forget.

The word parts in this activity can be used to make at least 44 words. I include only a portion of the words here so you can see how a child's paper might look at the conclusion of the activity:

1. Short Vowel Words	2. Long Vowel Words
chat	chase
check	chime
chin	choke
chop	chose
shack	shame
shut	shape
that	these
hick	whale
shop	shave
whip	white
when	while
then	shine

DISCOVERING CONSONANT BLENDS

Write the following words on the chalkboard before beginning this discovery activity:

Blends	Digraphs
*st*ack	**sh**op
*sk*ill	**ch**eck
*sl*ap	**wh**y
*bl*ed	**th**in
*br*at	**th**em

Read the words in both columns with the children. Ask them to study the words in both columns carefully to see if they can tell you the difference between consonant blends and consonant digraphs. As they offer explanations, help them discover that a digraph represents only one sound, but each consonant letter in a blend represents its own sound. To help them with this discovery, ask them such questions as, "If we added the letter *s* to the word *tack*, what word would we make? (*stack*)" "What would the word *skill* be if we took away the letter *s*? (*kill*)" "If we added the letter *s* to the word *hop*, would we get the word /s/ /hop/? (no)" Help them see that we can separate, add, or delete the letters in a consonant blend, and the sounds represented by all of the individual consonants do not change. However, the letters in a consonant digraph, if separated, represent a different sound individually than they do when those letters are together.

ACTIVITIES WITH CONSONANT BLENDS

Making Consonant Blend Words

Write the following letters and words on the chalkboard or type them on an activity sheet for a dyad group activity:

Consonants: s, b, p, c

tab	tack	tag	till	tub
tuck	tone	kill	kid	kit
lap	lid	lot	lip	lick
late	lice	lime	lack	led
rat	rag	red	rig	rim
rush	race	rake	rave	luck
lug	lace	lane	lam	lass
lock	log	rack		

Ask the children to make new words with consonant blends by adding the consonant *s*, *b*, *p*, or *c* to the words listed.

The new words that could be made are *stab, stack, stag, still, stub, stuck, stone, skill, skid, skit, slap, sled, slid, slot, slack, slip, slick, slate, slice, slime, black, bled, block, blot, brat, brag, bred, brig, brim, brush, brace, brake, brave, plot, pled, pluck, plug, place, plane, clip, clack, clam, clap, class, click, clock, clog, cluck, crack,* and *crag.*

Making New Words from Consonant Blends

Write the following words on the chalkboard or type them on an activity sheet for a dyad group activity:

crib	crock	crash	crest	crush
crate	crave	glad	gloss	globe
grip	grid	grim	grub	gruff
grace	grope	price	pride	probe
trot	trim	trip	track	trash
trace	frock	drip	drag	drug
drub	flap	fled	flip	flock
flog	flake	flame	smile	swell
swish	spot	span	spat	speck
spill	spin	spit	space	spine
spoke	scab	scat	scan	strap
strip	throb	thrush	shrub	shred
shrug	twin	twig	twill	twine

Begin this activity by asking the children such questions as "What would the word *crib* be without the *c?*" "What would the word *crock* be without the *c?*" "What would the word *crash* be without the *r?*" "What would the word *crash* be without the *c?*"

Ask the children to make new words from the words above by deleting various consonant letters. The following words could be made: *rib, rock, rash, cash, rest, rush, rate, cave, rave, lad, loss, lobe, rip, rid, rim, rub, ruff, race, rope, rice, ride, robe, rot, tot, rim, Tim, rip, tip, tack, rack, rash, race, rock, dip, rip, rag, dug, rug, rub, lap, fed, led, lip, lock, fog, log, lake, fake, fame, lame, mile, sell, well, wish, pot, pan, sat, pat, peck, pill, sill, sin, pin, sit, pit, pace, pine, poke, cab, sat, cat, can, trap, rap, trip, rip, rob, rush, rub, shed, red, rug, tin, twin, wig, till, will,* and *wine.*

SYLLABLE PATTERN ACTIVITY WITH BEGINNING CONSONANT BLENDS

The following cards are needed for the consonant digraphs activity:

fli	ve
sto	p
sto	ne
sla	ke
sla	me
bra	ce
bra	n
pla	g
pla	b
cri	ze
cri	d
gla	ss
gla	de

Key

italic letters (blue) = short vowel sound

boldface letters (green) = long vowel sound (go)

underlined letters (red) = silent (stop)

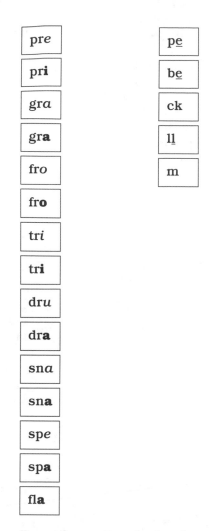

Procedures: Divide the class into dyad groups and give pencils and paper to the children in each group. Ask the children to make two column headings on their papers: "1. Long Vowel Words" and "2. Short Vowel Words." The words they construct should be written under the appropriate column headings.

Instructions to the children: The instructions for this activity are similar to those you used with single consonants and consonant digraphs. Children should be encouraged to say the vowel sound in the beginning word part first, then coarticulate the consonant next to the vowel with the vowel, and finally, coarticulate the first consonant with the second consonant and vowel to get the correct pronunciation of the beginning word element. Then they should search the word ending column for suitable endings—either an ending with a consonant, if the vowel sound is short, or an ending with a consonant followed by an *e*, if the vowel sound is long.

The dyad groups should be given a reasonable amount of time to make their word lists. At the end of the allotted time, each team should check with a dictionary to make sure all of the words they identified are spelled correctly.

The word parts in this activity can be used to make at least 64 words. I include only a portion of the words here so you can see how a child's paper might look at the conclusion of the activity.

1. Long Vowel Words	**2. Short Vowel Words**
stove	flip
stone	stop
slave	slap
brave	slam
brake	brag
brace	brass
plane	plan
crime	crib
glaze	glad
prize	press
pride	grab
grape	grass
froze	frog
tribe	trip
drape	drug
snake	snap
space	spell
flake	speck

DISCOVERING VOWEL TEAM PATTERNS

Vowel Digraphs and Diphthongs

Write the following words on the chalkboard:

1	**2**	**3**
oa	oi	ou
road	oil	out
soap	voice	loud
goat	join	sound
toast	point	count
boat	noise	house
load	choice	scout
coat	coin	mouse

Explain to the children that when we have two vowel letters representing one sound we call those letters a digraph. Tell them that the letters *oa* at the beginning of the first column of words comprise a vowel digraph. Tell the children that you are going to read the words in column 1 with them. Ask them to listen carefully to the vowel sound in each word as the words are read.

Read the words in column 1 with the children, and when you have finished, ask them to tell you the sound represented by the letters *oa*. Explain to them that you have underlined the *o* in these words with a green magic marker (I have bolded those letters), so they know that the long *o* vowel sound is heard. Also explain to them that you have underlined the *a* in these words with a red magic marker (I have underlined those letters), so they know that the letter *a* is silent. (Green means "go" and red means "stop." Green suggests to the children that they go ahead and say the name of the letter, and the red suggests that they stop and don't try to say a sound for that letter.)

Explain to the children that the letters *oi* and *ou* represent gliding vowel sounds (these are vowel diphthongs, but you may not want to use that word with the children). Ask them to read all of the words in column 2 with you and listen to the vowel sound in each word as they are read. Read the words in column 2 with the children, and when you are finished, ask them to tell you the sound represented by the letters *oi*. Tell them that the vowel sound in these words is neither long nor short so none of the letters have been underlined. However, if they remember the first word in the column (*oil*) they will be able to remember the sound represented by the letters *oi*. Ask them to say the word *oil* without saying the sound represented by the last letter (*l*), and they will be able to clearly hear the sound represented by the letters *oi*.

Ask the children to read all of the words in column 3 with you and listen to the vowel sound in each word as they are read. Read the words in column 3 with the children, and when you are finished, ask them to tell you the sound represented by the letters *ou*. Tell them that the vowel sound in these words is neither long nor short so letters have not been underlined. However, if they remember the first word in the column (*out*) they will be able to remember the sound represented by the letters *ou*. Ask them to say the word *out* without saying the sound represented by the last letter (*t*), and they will be able to clearly hear the sound represented by the letters *ou*.

You should continue this activity with other vowel digraphs: *ai (rain), ay (day), aw (lawn), au (sauce), ee (deep), ea (heat* and *head), oo (room* and *book), ew (blew), ue (blue),* and *ow (show),* and with other vowel diphthongs: *ow (cow)* and *oy (boy).* Notice that *ow* represents either a diphthong sound or a long vowel sound. Children should also be helped to discover the sound represented by the vowel trigraph *igh (night).*

Murmur Diphthong Vowel Teams

Write the following words on the chalkboard:

1	2	3	4	5
er	ir	ur	ar	or
her	first	burn	arm	for
herd	girl	curl	art	torn
verb	dirt	turn	car	storm
stern	third	nurse	dark	corn
term	bird	fur	shark	born
fern	shirt	purse	barn	short
germ	firm	hurt	farm	fork

Explain to the children that when we have a vowel letter followed by an *r*, those letters represent one murmuring vowel sound. (These sounds are called murmur diphthong sounds.) Tell them that all of the letter teams at the top of the columns represent murmuring vowel sounds. Tell them that you are going to read the words in the first three columns with them. Ask them to listen carefully to the vowel sound in each word as the words are read and tell you how those sounds are alike or different.

Read the words in columns 1, 2, and 3 with the children, and when you have finished, ask them to tell you the sound represented by the letters *er, ir,* and *ur*. They should conclude that all of these vowel teams represent the same sound, /ûr/.

Read the words in columns 4 and help the children discover that the vowel team *ar* represents the phoneme /ar/. Read the words in columns 5 and help the children discover that the vowel team *or* represents the phoneme /or/.

You should continue this activity with other murmur diphthongs: *are (care), air (chair), eer (deer),* and *ear (year).*

SYLLABLE PATTERN ACTIVITY INVOLVING OPEN, CLOSED, VCe, AND VOWEL TEAM SYLLABLES

Prepare cards for the following phonics elements. Make them large enough for all of the children in the classroom to see, put masking tape on the back of each element, and stick each element on the chalkboard:

1   **2**

1	2
b*a*	ck
n**o**	d<u>e</u>
ba<u>i</u>	b
b**o**	t
b**o**<u>a</u>	x
pr**o**	d
m*a*	n<u>e</u>
m**e**	n
ma<u>i</u>	k<u>e</u>
sh**e**	l<u>e</u>
m**o**<u>a</u>	g<u>e</u>
m**o**	<u>d</u>g<u>e</u>
ra<u>i</u>	<u>t</u>ch
r**a**	
r*a*	
b**a**	
b**o**	
m*a*	
m**o**	

Key

italic letters (blue) = short vowel sound

boldface letters (green) = long vowel sound (go)

underlined letters (red) = silent (stop)

Procedures: Divide the class into dyad groups and give pencils and paper to the children in each group. Ask the children to make four column headings on their papers: "1. Syllables Ending with Vowels," "2. Syllables Ending with Consonants," "3. Syllables Ending with Consonants Followed by an *e*," and "4. Vowel Team Syllables."

Instructions to the children: The instructions for this activity are similar to those you used with single consonants, consonant digraphs, and consonant blends. The task is to see how many words the dyad teams can read and write by taking the word parts from the first column and combining them with word parts from the second column. The word parts in column 1 are the beginnings of words and the word parts in column 2 are the endings of words. The words the children construct should be written under the appropriate column headings.

All of the vowel letters underlined in blue in column 1 represent short vowel sounds (those I have italicized). All of the vowel letters underlined in green (those I have bolded) in column 1 represent long vowel sounds. All of the letters in red (those I have underlined) in both columns 1 and 2 do not represent any sound at all.

You will need to help the children understand that when the phoneme /j/ occurs at the end of words, we spell that sound with the letters *ge.* So the *e* at the end of the *ge* helps the reader know that the vowel letter in that word is long and that the *g* represents /j/. Therefore, when we have a *dge* ending, the *d* lets the reader know that the vowel letter in that word is short, and the *ge* lets the reader know that the *g* represents /j/. The *tch* ending serves a similar function. The letter *t* lets the reader know that the vowel letter in the word is short, so it doesn't represent any sound, and the *ch* represents /ch/.

Children should be encouraged to say the vowel sound in the beginning word part first, then coarticulate the consonant next to the vowel with the vowel, and if there is another consonant unit in the word, that unit should be coarticulated with the second consonant and vowel to get the correct pronunciation of the beginning word element. Children should then search the word ending column for suitable endings. Some of the word parts in column 1 represent words by themselves and need no ending.

The dyad groups should be given a reasonable amount of time to make their word lists. At the end of the allotted time, each team should check with a dictionary to make sure all of the words they identified are spelled correctly.

The word parts in this activity can be used to make at least 47 words. I include only a portion of the words here so you can see how a child's paper might look at the conclusion of the activity:

1. Syllables Ending in Vowels	2. Syllables Ending in Consonants	3. Syllables Ending in Consonant + e	4. Vowel Team Syllables
no	badge	bake	bait
pro	box	bone	boat
me	match	make	maid
she	man	made	main
	mob	male	moan
	rat	rake	rain

Chapter 9

Learning to Read and Write Words of More than One Syllable

The activities presented in this part of the book are designed to help children read and write multisyllabic words. The keys to reading and writing words of more than one syllable are (1) understanding morphemic units in multisyllabic words; (2) understanding the schwa sound in unaccented syllables of American English speech; (3) understanding how vowel sounds are predicted in written language by syllable and vowel team patterns; and (4) perceiving the syllable boundaries in multisyllabic words.

Morphemes

Morphemes are the smallest unit of meaning in a word. In the word *unable* there are two morphemes: *un* (meaning "not") and *able* (meaning "capable"). Another way of saying that someone is *unable* to walk, is to say that they are *not capable* of walking.

Many multisyllabic words contain more than one morpheme. Word variants contain root words with an inflectional ending such as *s, es, er, est, ing,* and *ed.* Inflectional endings and root words are morphemes. Word derivatives contain root words with either a prefix, a suffix, or both a prefix and a suffix. Prefixes and suffixes are also morphemes, or units of meaning. If morphemes are recognized in written words, those words are more easily read by children. The more children are knowledgeable about morphemic units, the more they will use that knowledge to write words containing them.

The Schwa Sound

When we say two-syllable words, we usually accent (emphasize) one of them and do not accent the other. For example, in the word *alone,* the un-accented syllable is *a* and the accented syllable is *lone.* In the word *pilot,* the accented syllable is *pi* and the unaccented syllable is *lot.* In the accented syllable, the vowel represents the sound predicted by the syllable pattern. However, in the unaccented syllable, the vowel represents the schwa sound, /u/. In words of more than two syllables, accented and unaccented syllables are often alternated. For example, in the word *communication,* the first syllable is unaccented, the second is accented, the third is unaccented, the fourth is accented, and the last syllable is unaccented. The schwa sound is the vowel sound we hear in all of the unaccented syllables in that word, and the vowel in the accented syllables are predicted by the syllable pattern. If children are aware of the schwa sound in multisyllabic words, reading and writing words of more than one syllable is easier for them.

Syllable Patterns and Vowel Team Patterns

All of the activities designed to help children read and write single-syllable words will also help them read and write words of more than one syllable. These syllable and vowel team patterns occur in multisyllabic words, and a knowledge of them helps children read and write multisyllabic words. In particular, a knowledge of open syllables (syllables ending with vowels) really "pays off" when reading and writing words of more than one syllable. There are not many single-syllable words ending in vowel sounds, but there are a huge number of these syllables in multisyllabic words. For example, in the words **ti**ger, **no**tice, **fe**ver, **op**en, and **ba**con, the first syllable in each word ends in a vowel, is accented, and the vowel letter in those syllables represents its long sound.

Perceiving Syllable Boundaries

Knowing when written syllables end and begin is particularly important for reading and writing words of more than one syllable. You learned about how to perceive these boundaries yourself in the first section of the book. Teaching children how to identify the syllable boundaries in multisyllabic words helps them perceive the syllable patterns that are often difficult to perceive in such words, and provides an important key for word identification.

The activities presented in this part of the book are designed to help children (1) become aware of morphemic units, (2) become aware of the schwa sound, (3) apply their knowledge of syllable and vowel team patterns to the identification of multisyllabic words, and (4) become aware of syllable boundaries.

MAKING WORDS FROM MORPHEMES

Compound Words

Prepare cards for the following morphemes. Make them large enough for all of the children in the classroom to see, put masking tape on the back of each morpheme card, and stick each on the chalkboard.

1	2	**Key:** underline = schwa sound
milk	maid	
hand	man	
home	shake	
mail	stool	
	book	
	cart	
	cuff	
	bag	
	made	
	out	
	rail	
	box	
	s<u>o</u>me	

Procedures: Divide the class into dyad groups and give pencils and paper to the children in each group.

Instructions to the children: Instruct the children to see how many words their dyad teams can read and write by taking the root words from the first column and combining them with the root words from the second column.

If children have difficulty reading the root words in the first column, encourage them to first say the vowel sound in the word, then coarticulate the consonant next to the vowel with the vowel, isolate the ending sound, and blend the sounds together to get the correct pronunciation of the word. After the children have identified the words in the first column, they should then search the second column for a suitable ending, or endings.

The dyad groups should be given a reasonable amount of time to make words. At the end of the allotted time, each team should check with a dictionary to make sure all of the words they identified are spelled correctly.

The words the children could construct are: *milkmaid, milkman, milkshake, milkstool, handmaid, handshake, handbook, handcart, handcuff, handbag, handmade, handsome, handout, handrail, homework, homemade, homesick, mailbox,* and *mailman.*

In order for the children to construct words in this activity, they need to be knowledgeable about both syllable and vowel team patterns. Furthermore, they need to be able to coarticulate phonemes to sound out words. Therefore, it is an effective tool to use to help reinforce and apply phonics knowledge.

Word Variants and Derivatives

Prepare cards for the following morphemes. Make them large enough for all of the children in the classroom to see, put masking tape on the back of each morpheme card, and stick each on the chalkboard.

1	2	**Key:** underline = schwa sound
fast	er	
dark	ing	
wait	est	
start	ed	
sick	ness	
bash	ful	
grace	ment	

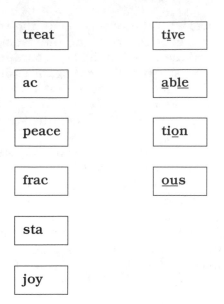

Procedures: Divide the class into dyad groups and give pencils and paper to the children in each group.

Instructions to the children: Instruct the children to see how many words their dyad teams can read and write by taking the root words from the first column and combining them with the inflectional endings or suffixes from the second column. Help them understand that the underlined vowels in the inflectional endings or suffixes represent the schwa sound. You may need to help the children with the *tion* and *able* suffixes. Explain to them that the *ti* in the *tion* suffix represents /sh/ and the *o* represents the schwa sound. The *tion* suffix is therefore pronounced /shun/. The *le* at the end of multisyllabic words represents the /ul/ sound, and the *a* in the suffix *able* represents the schwa sound; therefore, the *able* suffix is pronounced with two schwa sounds: /u/-/bul/.

The dyad groups should be given a reasonable amount of time to make words. At the end of the allotted time, each team should check with a dictionary to make sure all of the words they identified are spelled correctly.

The words the children could construct are *faster, fastest, fasted, darker, darkest, waiting, waited, starting, started, sickness, bashful, graceful, treatment, active, treatable, peaceable, fraction, station,* and *joyous.*

This activity could be used many times, with different root words, inflectional endings, and suffixes.

MAKING WORDS WITH SYLLABLES

Prepare cards for the following syllables. Make them large enough for all of the children in the classroom to see, put masking tape on the back of each syllable card, and stick each on the chalkboard.

1	2	**Key:** underline = schwa sound
sat	in	
sam	da	
so	ple	
sad	ver	
sil	dle	
sel	en	
sev	fish	
sig	lent	
sim	nal	
si	ter	
sis	vor	
sud	tal	
fa	den	
fau	ble	
	cet	

Procedures: Divide the class into dyad groups and give pencils and paper to the children in each group.

Instructions to the children: Instruct the children to see how many words their dyad teams can read and write by taking the syllables from the first column and combining them with the syllables from the second column. The children are to use their knowledge of syllable patterns and vowel team patterns to determine the vowel sounds represented by the vowel letters in the syllables in the first column. The underlined vowels in the syllables in the second column represent the schwa sound.

This activity should help children become aware of the schwa sound in unaccented syllables. Furthermore, the activity should help them gain insights into syllable boundaries, as well as help them apply their knowledge of syllable patterns in determining the vowel sounds in syllables.

The dyad groups should be given a reasonable amount of time to make words. At the end of the allotted time, each team should check with a dictionary to make sure all of the words they identified are spelled correctly.

The words the children could construct are *satin, soda, sample, saddle, silver, selfish, seven, signal, simple, silent, sister, sudden, fatal, favor, fable, faucet.*

After the words have been constructed, they could be organized into the following groups:

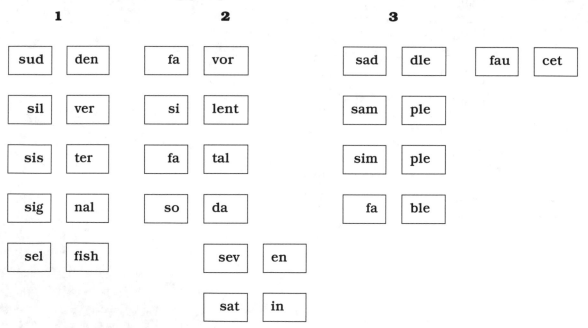

1

		2			**3**			
sud	den	fa	vor		sad	dle	fau	cet
sil	ver	si	lent		sam	ple		
sis	ter	fa	tal		sim	ple		
sig	nal	so	da		fa	ble		
sel	fish	sev	en					
		sat	in					

With the words organized into these groups, you can help children discover the basic principles for identifying syllable boundaries that you learned in the first section of the book. **Principle one:** If there are two consonant units separating "sounding" vowels, the first unit ends after the first consonant unit (group 1). **Principle two:** If there is only one consonant unit separating "sounding" vowels, the first syllable will often end after the vowel; however, sometimes it ends after the consonant (group 2). **Principle three:** If a word ends in an *le*, the last syllable begins with the consonant preceding the *le* (group 3). The first syllable in the word *faucet* is accented and contains a vowel team; therefore, the vowel sound in the first syllable is determined by the vowel team pattern, and the vowel sound in the second syllable represents the schwa sound.

This activity may be used many times with different multisyllabic words. It is a very effective activity. It helps children learn important concepts regarding multisyllabic words. The activity is challenging for children and provides them with considerable practice applying phonics knowledge for the identification of multisyllabic words.

Answers to Reviews and Self-Evaluation Tests

These reviews let you know how well you have mastered the content presented in this self-instruction program. If you seek to do well, you will realize your goal. Work to achieve 100% on each review. Good luck.

Review 1 **1.** receptive, written **2.** grapheme **3.** translating written words into speech **4.** the smallest unit of sound within a word. **5.** No. A grapheme is the unit of written text that represents a phoneme. Sometimes a grapheme is one letter and sometimes it is more than one letter. **6.** 44 **7.** five **8.** five: a th l e te

Review 2 **1.** *y* and *w* **2.** they begin words or syllables **3.** The letters *c, x,* and *q* have no sounds of their own. Other consonant letters predictably represent the phonemes these letters represent. **4.** *ch, sh, th, wh, ng* **5.** a two-letter grapheme representing one consonant phoneme

Review 3 **1.** lips, tongue, teeth, gums, palate, and vocal cords **2.** voiceless **3.** vibrating our vocal cords **4.** equivalent **5.** /b/ and /p/, /v/ and /f/, /z/ and /s/, /d/ and /t/, /g/ and /k/, /th/ and /th/, /w/ and /hw/, /zh/ and /sh/, /j/ and /ch/ **6.** Consonant phonemes are used in the initial and/or final position of syllables and single-syllable words.

Review 4 **1.** The letter *b* reliably predicts the phoneme /b/ in written words, the letter *d* reliably predicts the phoneme /d/ in written words, and the letter *f* reliably predicts the phoneme /f/ in written words. **2.** *m, t* (examples: *comb, subtle*) **3.** When the grapheme *c* is followed by an *e, i,* or *y*, it represents the phoneme /s/. All other times it represents the phoneme /k/. **4.** /k/ (76% of the time) **5.** /sh/ (examples: *ocean, social*) **6.** Unless *g* is followed by an *e,i,* or *y*, it represents its own sound. When *g* is followed by an *e, i,* or *y*, it usually represents /j/, but not always. However, when *ge* and *dge* occur at the end of words or syllables, they represent /j/. **7.** /g/ (70% of the time) **8.** is silent **9.** represents /g/ **10.** is silent (example: *gnat*) represents /g/ (examples: *guide, guess*)

Review 5   **1.** The graphemes *h, j, k, l,* and *m* reliably predict the phonemes /h/, /j/, /k/, /l/, and /m/, respectively.   **2.** represents a phoneme in the final position of a syllable or word.   **3.** appears as the first letter of a word (examples: *honor, honest*), and when it follows the consonants *k, r,* and *g* at the beginning of words (examples: *khaki, rhine, ghost*)   **4.** *sh, th, wh, ch*   **5.** represents a phoneme in the final position of a syllable or word.   **6.** is followed by an *n* at the beginning of words (examples: *know, knee*)   **7.** it precedes another consonant within a word or syllable (examples: *chalk, should*)

Review 6   **1.** The graphemes *n, p,* and *r* reliably predict the phonemes /n/, /p/, and /r/, respectively.   **2.** occurs in words more frequently   **3.** *ng* as in *sing, ph* as in *phone*   **4.** the letter *p* occurs at the beginning of words followed by an *s, t,* or *n* (examples: *psalm, ptomaine, pneumonia*)   **5.** at the beginning of words or syllables (examples: *run, already*)   **6.** a part of the vowel   **7.** *u*   **8.** /kw/ (examples: *quit, require*), /k/ (examples: *unique, opaque*)   **9.** /s/   **10.** at the end of words   **11.** /z/ (examples: *dogs, drums*), /s/ (examples: *sits, cups*)   **12.** /z/ (examples: *does, sues, flies, tubes*), /s/ (examples: *ropes, plates, makes*)

Review 7   **1.** *th*   **2.** /shun/ (example: *action*), /chun/ (example: *mention*)   **3.** silent (examples: *debut, listen*)   **4.** very reliable   **5.** it is never found at the end of words without an *e* after it   **6.** *r* (examples: *write, wrist*)   **7.** it follows the vowels *a, e,* or *o* (examples: *lawn, blew, town*)   **8.** /ks/ (example: *fix*), /gz/ (example: *exam*)   **9.** it is not used to begin words or syllables (examples: *myth, dry, rhyme*), and when it is preceded by a vowel (examples: *play, toy*)   **10.** /s/ as in *waltz*, /zh/ as in *azure*   **11.** *s* (example: *hounds*)

Review 8   **1.** *ng*   **2.** When a prefix ending with an *n* occurs before a root word beginning with a *g* (*ingest*), readers might think they see the *ng* digraph. When a *ge* or *gi* grapheme occurs at the ending of a word to represent /j/ and the letter before that ending is *n* (*range, changing*), readers might think they see the *ng* digraph. This situation, however, should not be confused with the situation in which vowel-beginning endings are added to root words ending in the *ng* digraph (*stronger, youngest*)   **3.** /th/, /th/   **4.** When *th* is preceded by or follows another consonant letter (*tenth, three*), the *th* represents the voiceless /th/   **5.** /k/ (example: *chemical*), /sh/ (example: *machine*)   **6.** end, 100, short   **7.** The digraph *sh* consistently represents the phoneme /sh/ as in *shoe*   **8.** The digraph *wh* represents the phoneme /hw/ (*white*) about 90% of the time, and it represents the phoneme /h/ (*whole*) about 10% of the time.   **9.** /ng+k/ (example: *sink*)

Review 9   **1.** Consonant digraphs are two letters representing one phoneme. Consonant blends are two or more consonant letters representing two or more consonant phonemes. The letters comprising consonant digraphs should never be separated when separating syllables or sounding out words because they represent one phoneme. However, the letters representing consonant blends can be separated because each letter represents a separate phoneme.   **2.** Any word containing *thr* or *shr* in the initial position (*three, shrub*), or any word containing *nch* or *ngth* in the final position (*lunch, length*) is acceptable.

Review 10   **1.** The letter *y* represents vowel phonemes by itself, and it is also used with other vowel letters to form vowel digraphs and vowel diphthongs. The letters *w, r,* and *gh* are also used as part of vowel teams (examples: *cow, bird, fight*).   **2.** the same phonemes the letter *i* represents when it occurs in words (examples: *myth, my, rhyme*)   **3.** either /e/ or /i/.   **4.** When the letter *r* is preceded by vowel letters, the vowel letters and the *r* become one vowel grapheme (examples: *first, hair, bear, hurt*)

Review 11   **1.** voiceless   **2.** /a/ *at*; /ā/ *ate*; /e/ *edge*; /ē/ *eat*; /i/ *it*; /ī/ *ice*; /o/ *ox*; /ō/ *oat*; /u/ *up*; /ū/ *use*; /o͞o/ *moon*; /oo/ *book*; /oi/ *boy*; /ou/ *out*; /ûr/ *first*; /ar/ *car*; /or/ *for*; /âr/ *bear*; /êr/ *year*

Review 12   **1.** macron   **2.** the VCe pattern (examples: *bone, wine*) and the open syllable pattern (examples: *no, we*)   **3.** short vowel sounds   **4.** *e, ve*

Review 13   **1.** breve   **2.** short, long   **3.** The closed syllable pattern (*can, camp*) predicts that a single vowel grapheme will represent the short vowel phoneme. Closed syllables end in consonant phonemes.   **4.** are not (Murmur diphthongs end in vowel phonemes.)   **5.** *ost, old, oll, olt, ind, ild*   **6.** phonemes in the same way the letter *i* represents them. In closed syllables it represents the short sound of *i* (*myth*), and in VCe and open syllables it represents the long sound of *i* (*rhyme, my*).

Review 14   **1.** a vowel and some other letter representing one vowel phoneme.   **2.** a vowel team syllable   **3.** murmur diphthong   **4.** /ûr/   **5.** *oi* (*coin*), *oy* (*boy*), *ou* (*out*), *ow* (*cow*)   **6.** *oi oy, ou ow*   **7.** long *o* (*show*), diphthong /ou/ (*how*)   **8.** The *ou* vowel team represents the /ou/ diphthong phoneme only about 60% of the time. It represents /u/ (*country*) about 18% of the time. It represents /ō/ (*soul*) about 10% of the time, and the remaining 12% of the time it represents /o͞o/ (*group*), /o/ (*sought*), and /oo/ (*should*).   **9.** two letters representing one vowel phoneme.   **10.** *ai, ay, ee,* and *oa*   **11.** /ē/ (*meat*), /e/ (*bread*) **12.** /o/ (*saw* and *sauce*)   **13.** /o͞o/ (*moon*), /oo/ (*book*)   **14.** /o͞o/ (*new, due*), /yo͞o/ (*few, cue*)   **15.** The digraph *ey* represents /ē/ only 70% of the time, and it represents /ā/ about 30% of the time. The digraph *ie* represents /ē/ (*piece*) only about 65% of the time, it represents /ī/ (*pie*) about 26% of the time, and it represents /e/ (*friend*) about 9% of the time. The digraph *ui* represents /o͞o/ (*fruit*) only 67% of the time, and it represents /i/ (*build*) about 33% of the time. The digraph _ei_ is not too reliable. When _ei_ and _eigh_ are considered together, they represent /ā/ about 52% of the time (_vein, weigh_). About 32% of the time, _ei_ represents /ē/ (_seize_), and the rest of the time it represents other phonemes (_heifer_, for example).

Review 15   **1.** A syllable is the smallest part of the word containing one vowel sound. It is the smallest unit of pronunciation.   **2.** the number of syllables in the word   **3.** we can feel the vibration of our vocal cords as we say syllables   **4.** We study syllabication so we can help young readers find the syllable patterns in multisyllabic words they don't recognize so they can use their phonics knowledge to identify them.   **5.** When we stress or emphasize a syllable in a multisyllabic word, that syllable is said to be accented. The phoneme represented by the vowel grapheme in an accented syllable is predicted by its syllable pattern. When we don't accent a syllable, the vowel in that syllable often represents the /u/ or schwa sound. However, the schwa sound is not used when unaccented syllables end in _c, y, ge_, or a murmur diphthong. Words of more than three syllables can have two accents—a primary accent and a secondary accent. These words generally follow the alternating principle; that is, if one syllable is accented, the next one will be unaccented, and so on.   **6.** /ī/ (_deny_), /ē/ (_baby_)   **7.** The accent usually falls on or within the first word of a compound word.   **8.** The accent usually falls on the root word.   **9.** In two-syllable words the accent is usually placed on the first syllable unless the word begins with a prefix.
10. The _ed_ inflectional ending is a syllable when it is preceded by a _t_ or a _d._
11. In most multisyllabic words ending in _tion, sion, ic_, and _sive_, the primary accent falls on the syllable preceding these endings.   **12.** In most multisyllabic words ending in _ary, ist, ize, ism, fy, tude, y, ate_, and _tory_, the primary accent falls on the syllable before the syllable preceding these endings.
13. In most multisyllabic words ending in _al, an, ent/ant, ous, ar, ence/ance, able/ible, age, tive_, and _ency/ancy_, the primary accent falls on the syllable before the syllable preceding these endings **if** there is only one consonant before the suffix. If there are two consonants, the primary accent falls on the syllable preceding the ending.

Review 16   **1.** We begin the task of locating syllable boundaries by determining which vowel letters in a word represent vowel sounds.   **2.** We must know that vowel teams represent one phoneme; the _e_ vowel in VCe syllables is silent; the _e_ in _dge_ and _ge_ graphemes at the end of words is silent; the letter _y_ represents a vowel phoneme when it isn't used to begin words or syllables; _le_ at the end of multisyllabic words represents the syllable /ul/; the letters _ci_ and _ti_ when followed by vowels (_facial, direction_) represent vowel phonemes; and when the letters _gi_ and _ge_ are followed by vowels (_legion, pigeon_), those letters represent the phoneme /j/.   **3.** We look at the number of consonant units between the vowels representing phonemes. There will be either one or two consonant units. If there are two or more consonant units between vowels representing phonemes, the first syllable ends after the first consonant unit. If there is one consonant unit between vowels representing phonemes, divide the syllable after the first vowel and pronounce the word. If it doesn't make sense, divide the syllable after the consonant unit.

Answers to the Self-Evaluation Pretest

1. c　**2.** c　**3.** d　**4.** d　**5.** e　**6.** e　**7.** b　**8.** e　**9.** e　**10.** e
11. a　**12.** a　**13.** b　**14.** b　**15.** c　**16.** b　**17.** b　**18.** e　**19.** b　**20.** e
21. b　**22.** b　**23.** e　**24.** e　**25.** c　**26.** a　**27.** d　**28.** e　**29.** d　**30.** d
31. c　**32.** d　**33.** e　**34.** c　**35.** b　**36.** b　**37.** b　**38.** d　**39.** c　**40.** a
41. d　**42.** c　**43.** d*　**44.** d*　**45.** d*　**46.** a*　**47.** b　**48.** d　**49.** c　**50.** b
*Explanations of certain answers:

43. The grapheme *ti* represents /ch/ (*attention*) as does the grapheme *ch* in the word *chin*. The grapheme *ti* also represents /sh/ (*appreciation*) just as the graphemes *sh* and *s* do in the words *shop* and *sure*.

44. The grapheme *ci* represents /sh/ (*facial*) just as the graphemes *sh* and *s* do in the words *shoot* and *sugar*. The grapheme *ci* also represents /si/ (*city*) just as the grapheme *si* does in the word *sit*.

45. The grapheme *ge* represents /ge/ (*get*) just as the grapheme *gue* represents that phoneme in the word *guest*. The grapheme *ge* also represents /je/ (*gem*) just as the grapheme *je* does in the word *jet*. The grapheme *ge* also represents /j/ (*rage*) just as the grapheme *di* does in the word *soldier*.

46. The grapheme *ce* represents /s/ (*fence*) just as the grapheme *s* represents that sound in the word *sign*.

Answers to the Self-Evaluation Posttest

1. e　**2.** c　**3.** c　**4.** c　**5.** d　**6.** d　**7.** e　**8.** e　**9.** b　**10.** e
11. a　**12.** a　**13.** b　**14.** a　**15.** e　**16.** b　**17.** b　**18.** e　**19.** b　**20.** d
21. b　**22.** b　**23.** e　**24.** e　**25.** c　**26.** a　**27.** d　**28.** e　**29.** d　**30.** b.
31. c　**32.** d　**33.** e　**34.** b　**35.** c　**36.** b　**37.** c　**38.** d　**39.** e　**40.** a
41. d　**42.** e　**43.** d*　**44.** d*　**45.** d*　**46.** a*　**47.** b　**48.** c　**49.** c　**50.** b
Explanations of certain answers:

43. The grapheme *ti* represents /ch/ (*mention*) as does the grapheme *ch* in the word *choose*. The grapheme *ti* also represents /sh/ (*notion*) just as the graphemes *sh* and *ch* do in the words *wish* and *machine*.

44. The grapheme *ci* represents /sh/ (*racial*) just as the graphemes *sh* and *si* do in the words *sharp* and *session*. The grapheme *ci* also represents /si/ (*cinder*) just as the grapheme *si* does in the word *sip*.

45. The The grapheme *ge* represents /ge/ (*get*) just as the grapheme *gue* represents that phoneme in the word *guess*. The grapheme *ge* also represents /je/ (*gentle*) just as the grapheme *je* does in the word *jello*. The grapheme *ge* also represents /j/ (*huge*) just as the grapheme *j* does in the word *jump*.

46. The grapheme *ce* represents /s/ (*dance*) just as the grapheme *s* represents that sound in the word *single*.

Index